What others are saying about this book

John Corey was an ordinary man who did extraordinary things because of a God-given vision and a stubborn will to see it through. This book is at times plain and simple, down-to-earth, while other times it soars up to heaven. It captures the heart and soul of old school missionaries who didn't know the meaning of "short-term." Crossing the Atlantic on a freighter, traveling in Africa from village to village on a mule, getting mail every 4-6 weeks, dealing with poisonous snakes and no running water or indoor bathroom. It's a story of raising children who came to regard Africa as their home; a story of what missions once was that captures the heart of what missions will always be. John Corey's was a life full of joys and sorrows. I was deeply moved by the account of his death, before which he spoke personally with and blessed every child and grandchild. In a time when we think too much about inheritances and too little about heritage, John and Jeanette Corey have left their family a remarkable heritage. Reunion awaits in a far better world. Read this book and learn the calling, costs, joys and ultimate rewards of missions, and of living with an eternal perspective.

Randy Alcorn, New York Times bestselling author, with over 40 books including *Heaven* and *Safely Home*

I love this line from John's book, "Among all the people on the planet, I may be the last one He considered calling into His service." It's an enjoyable, insightful and at times emotional read into the life and times of another era. John's story redefines calling, hardship, sacrifice, joy and community all bedded in a deep faith. Enjoy reading what God can do through ordinary people like all of us.

Bruce Johnson, president SIM USA, the global mission

I loved this story. A very ordinary man, but extraordinarily committed to knowing God and simply doing what Jesus said. It is only this simple but profound faith that can bring change to this broken world.

Jonathan Martin, author *Giving Wisely* and *Breaking the King Saul Syndrome*, pastor Good Shepherd Community Church

As a teacher of missions, I am always moved when I read and then tell my students the stories of missionary heroes, men and women with great faith who have launched out to carry the gospel of Christ to reach lost people no matter what the cost. John Corey has become one of my missionary heroes and this book documents why. Before I knew John's life story, he was first a friend and SIM colleague whose faithfulness to attend our SIM prayer meetings encouraged me when we first moved to Portland, Oregon. But soon John, a so-called missionary "retiree," became so much more to me as I learned about his ongoing travels to teach and mentor pastors in Liberia and Siberia. Even after his cancer diagnosis, he continued to travel, challenging pastors to read, study and preach the Word. As his days of travel were ending, I was humbled when John asked me to take up the mantle of directing the Romans Project. This ministry has been a great blessing and challenge as I have witnessed John's vision expand now into 19 countries in Africa and Asia. It has been my practice to tell John's story to all of my classes; now others can read it in this book which I will recommend and which will have a prominent place on my office shelf full of the biographies of missionary heroes.

Dr. Rick Calenberg, International Director of Romans Project, professor of World Missions and Intercultural Studies, Dallas Theological Seminary

You don't want to miss this book! Every church member who knows a missionary, every Bible school student who wants to be a missionary, and every Christian who wants to know how God builds His kingdom should read this exciting, poignant, challenging history of three mission fields, and how God used one family to grow His local churches in unlikely places. John and Jeanette Corey's story is a glorious reminder to all of us that God is faithful and can do extraordinary things with ordinary people.
Christine Schneider, author of *In the Shadow of the Cathedral* and *Goodness for God's Sake,* a former missionary to Austria.

ANY OL' BUSH
WILL DO

Special thanks to

Jim Morud for the extensive hours interviewing John; for compiling his memoirs into an enjoyable read and documenting his life story, which points to his Savior, Jesus Christ.

Laura Castien who transcribed extensive recordings of John Corey's memoirs.

ANY OL' BUSH WILL DO

THE LIFE STORY OF JOHN COREY

AS TOLD TO JIM MORUD

To Jeanette,
my beloved and perfect wife for me,
the one who somehow continued loving me,

I love you,
John

x

Dedication

I write this to encourage each of you,
my beloved grandchildren,
Caleb, Alek, Isaiah, Marisa, Luke, Joseph,
Kaylyn, Seth, Isaac, Kyla, David, Malia,
Hannah, Rachael, Ian, Michael, Nathan, Josiah

The work goes on, but I can sense my part in it is finished. Growing tumors permeate my body. The doctors have told me my fight against cancer is over. And I know that my part in the race of life is also over. I have sought to stretch for the tape my whole life but this is my final breath and lunge.

"...the time of my departure has come. I have fought the good fight, I have finished the course, I have kept the faith; in the future there is laid up for me the crown of righteousness, which the Lord, the righteous Judge, will award to me on that day; and not only to me, but also to all who have loved His appearing." 2 Tim. 4:6-8[1]

I am holding out for a final gathering together of all the family around me, so I can touch each one and bless each one. My precious grandchildren, while I am close to finishing the race God put before me, each one of you still has some of your race to run. Sanctify Jesus Christ as Lord in your hearts and live a life fully committed to Him. Oh my dear ones, this book is written for you. Prepare your minds for action, keep sober in spirit, fix your hope completely on the grace to be brought to you at the resurrection of Jesus Christ.

I love you very much.
G'pa

Contents

Forward

Scott Gilchrist

I will never forget September 18, 2012, as my wife Kristi and I entered the home of our dear friends, John and Jeanette Corey. Jeanette greeted us warmly and thanked us for coming. She said that John had been mostly unresponsive for the past 24 hours. He had been suffering with multiple myeloma for over a decade, and now his time of departure was drawing near.

As we walked into the living room where John was lying on his hospital bed we didn't know what to expect. But then John opened his eyes, obviously recognizing me, and said, "Look who's here!" I was thrilled to see his cognizant smile and said, "I bring you greetings from Africa, John."

I had just returned from speaking to about 1400 pastors in Ghana, West Africa. We had gotten news on the previous Friday via email that John was very near his home-going. I was traveling with Romans Project director, Rick Calenberg, my son Jess and three sons-in-law. Pastor Momo Senah from Liberia was also in the van with us when we got the news.

John had challenged Momo two and a half years earlier to give himself to studying the gospel of Jesus Christ by repeatedly reading the Book of Romans twenty times and copying it out by hand. He urged Momo not only to do this himself, but also to challenge other pastors to do it. Momo took John's challenge seriously and he followed through on it. To aid his study, John gave Momo an MP3 player loaded with over a hundred messages from the Book of Romans that I had previously presented from our pulpit at Southwest Bible Church in Portland, Oregon. Momo had since urged many other Liberian pastors to do the same, and soon hundreds of pastors were studying Romans in this way.

Momo Senah sharing about the Romans Project

Like John, I had grown to love Momo. I was deeply moved when, upon hearing the news regarding John's grave condition, his eyes brimmed full with tears. We decided immediately to film a video to send to John on his deathbed. But try as we may, the video greeting we filmed would not send through the internet. So on that following Monday afternoon, as I greeted John in his living room, I also said to him, "I want you to hear from Momo." I opened my laptop and showed John the video greeting from Momo expressing his love and appreciation for the discipleship that John had given him.

About a minute into that two-minute greeting, John rested his head back on the pillow and wept tears of joy. Not knowing how much strength he had left to listen, I gave him brief greetings from other African pastors and told him about their hunger to be taught the Word of God and of my joy in teaching them. I asked John if I could read a portion of Romans 8. In his typically resolute manner, he asked, "Why not all of it?" I smiled and said, "Okay!"

As I read the 39 verses of Romans 8, I can't recall ever hearing that chapter speaking so poignantly to me. I have been comforted and have comforted others by reading it many times in hospital rooms and on other critical occasions, but as I read it again to John, the truth and the life of those words seemed to jump off the pages of my Bible. John was listening intently while every verse spoke directly to each one of us in the room. When I had finished reading, John looked at me and said, "What part of it would you have left out?" I couldn't help laughing. It was so typical of John to want to hear God's Word in its entirety. We prayed together and I reluctantly left that living room, realizing I probably would not see my brother alive again this side of heaven.

Within hours John went home to be with his Lord. He had lived his life well and the Lord had used him mightily in both East Africa and West Africa, as well as in Eastern Russia. He would be the first to say that he was whisked into God's presence, not because he was good enough or had worked hard enough to go there, but because he has a Savior, holy, innocent, and undefiled, who has entered heaven as a forerunner for him.

John's legacy lives on in many ways through the countless people he helped to trust and follow Jesus Christ, the outworking of what is now called The Romans Project. When I had shared with him a Bible study method that I had learned from my mentor, Dr. John Mitchell, John jumped right on it. It meant reading Romans and other Bible books twenty times and then writing them out by hand. Even though he had been studying and teaching from the Scriptures for decades himself, John loved both the challenge and the simplicity he saw in this method. He also saw a workable way of grounding untaught African pastors in the Word of God.

In 2010 John launched The Romans Project, which God continues to bless by effectively equipping thousands of pastors and church leaders in twelve African nations, and still counting. As with Pastor Momo, they have committed themselves to reading, writing, studying and preaching from the Book of Romans through this simple approach. God continues to transform leaders and whole congregations far beyond what John saw before the Lord took him home. He rejoiced at the news of how God was using The Romans Project while he was still here and his heart burned to see still more African church leaders carrying the torch long after he was gone.

Jim Morud, the teller of John's story, traveled three times with John to Russia. He has retold John's stories in this book, *Any Ol' Bush Will Do*. Jim captured John's self-styled "ordinariness" and his passion for pointing out God's glory in common places. I am sure you will find yourself thanking God, as I have done in reading it, for using John Corey to show you the glory of God in the life of a humble, ordinary man fully surrendered to Him. My prayer is that you also will be stirred and encouraged to give your life, your time, your abilities and energies to our Lord Jesus Christ.

If you would like to learn more about this ongoing ministry, please go to www.romansproject.org.

May God richly bless you.
Scott Gilchrist

June 2016

1

Unlikely Places and People

I once met a demon-possessed tax collector named Bongaow in Liberia. As you might expect from a man in his distressed state, he was neither a good nor just tax collector. His disposition did not mix well with his profession. On second thought, maybe it did. Tax collectors are not known for their charming qualities. Bongaow's home life was no better than his work life. By Liberian standards he was rich, and he had three wives, but he was not a happy man. His wives did not get along with each other and he couldn't escape their constant bickering. When his head wife suddenly died, Bongaow thought he might catch a breather from his hectic existence. But it only got worse. One of the evil spirits that was haunting him started mimicking her voice, constantly ordering him about.

"That's not your money!" the demon shouted, echoing the same charge that his head wife had always hurled at him. "It's mine! It's not for you!"

Day and night, the demons were driving him crazy. When he put on his clothing in the morning, his dead wife's voice ordered him to take off what he'd put on and wear something else. He planted a rice garden and the voice ordered him to pull up all the new shoots. He couldn't walk down the street without hearing those voices telling him to do something strange. He lived in an agitated state of mind.

Bongaow went back and forth to medicine men who kept bilking him, selling him all kinds of phony remedies. They sold him expensive potions and charms. He stuck fetishes under his floor and in his outside toilet. But nothing helped. Even in the restroom, he could find no rest.

Bongaow heard about a Bible study in Kolahun. He didn't know what it was all about, but when he went there he realized that he no longer heard those voices. So he kept coming back.

My wife, Jeanette, and I were missionaries serving with SIM in Liberia. A Liberian pastor named William Varney was leading that study. When I met Bongaow there, he told me about his miserable life, how he was plagued by constant harassment, except for when he had come to the Bible study. That was the only time in many years that he had not heard those dreadful voices.

I shared the gospel with him, explaining that if he would receive Christ in his life, God would deliver him from the demons because they cannot dwell where He dwells. Bongaow thought about it for a few more miserable days and then he came back to me. He said he was ready to be set free. I led him in a simple prayer of repentance from sin and acceptance of Christ. Then we went to his home where I instructed him to toss every fetish and every bottle of magic brew into the toilet. He was reluctant to destroy the bottles because he said they were worth a lot. His greed still had a grip on him, but I told him the bottles had to go because they too had been devoted to Satan. Bongaow had a mournful look on his face as he dumped the bottles down the hole.

I asked him if he could still hear the demons. He said, "I still hear 'em yet." I started singing hymns and reading from the Scriptures, rebuking the demons. After a couple hours of this, I asked him again if he could hear them. He answered, "I don't hear 'em now."

I told him, "You've accepted Christ. But Jesus said when demons go out of a person they will return with seven worse demons, so if you don't fill your mind with the truth, you will be bound again by lies."

I gave him a simple New Life Bible and told him to begin reading in the Gospel of John. When I returned in a few days, I asked him if he could still hear the demon voices.

"I still hear 'em yet," he replied.

I asked him if he had been reading his Bible.

"I forgot," he answered. His mind had gotten so degraded through years of demonic tyranny his thinking had become jumbled.

Bongaow took a two-week trip to Monrovia and when he came back to Kolahun he was a mess all over again. I asked him, "Did you read from your Bible?"

Again he answered, "I forgot to take it with me."

Shortly before we went home on furlough, I asked Pastor Varney to look after Bongaow, making sure he was daily reading from the Word. When we returned, Bongaow was peaceful. I could still see the lingering mental effects on him from all the years he had lived in spiritual bondage. He still looked lethargic, but he no longer heard those pesky voices. Even if they were still shouting at him, he couldn't hear them anymore. By reading God's Word, his ear had been trained to hear only the voice of the Good Shepherd. Though battered and embattled, he was finally a free man.

God has called Jeanette and me to serve His people in two African nations that have been torn apart by war. It has been nearly fifty years since we first went out to Africa. After we had to leave Africa, I found myself serving Him in post-communist Russia. In many ways, Ethiopia, Liberia and Russia collectively remind me of men like Bongaow. As Jesus looked at the masses when He walked the earth, He saw that they were downcast and distressed, like sheep without a shepherd. He still looks at the nations in this way. He can see a Bongaow in every crowd, in every country, and in every face.

He also sees me. Among all the people on the planet, I may be the last one He considered calling into His service. I am an ordinary man by every definition of the word. But maybe that's why I saw hope for a man like Bongaow. I knew that if God could call me into His service, He could reach anyone. Missionaries are usually good at learning foreign languages, or at least they are good at speaking their own. I speak neither very well. Missionaries are either good Bible teachers or good caregivers. I struggled to make C's in Bible school. It takes me hours to prepare a simple Bible lesson. And I would rather be alone in my workshop than entertaining an endless stream of people who want my help. This is what I am like in the flesh.

I am like my mother. I grew up in a family of ten children on a wooded farm on the Olympic Peninsula of Washington State. We worked hard to eke out a living. With all those kids to care for, my mother was constantly busy. We were all busy. Once in a while a neighbor would drop by our house. Hearing a knock at the door, I remember her sighing and saying, "Oh dear, what now?" But she would drop whatever she was doing, and by the time she had opened the door for her guests, she was smiling and joyfully inviting them to come in.

My mother was a devoted Christian, and I thought at the time that she was being hypocritical. But through the years I have come to see the contrast between my own sin nature and my new nature in Christ. I now understand that during her short walk to the front door, she surrendered her flesh to the Lord so that her guests would be greeted instead by Jesus at her door.

My dad was radically converted to Christ and he lived radically for Him. He read and studied and memorized God's Word so well that he had a scripture for every occasion. He used to say," The Lord has not given the same abilities to all believers, but He has a place of service for everyone who is available to Him."

I've never been overly concerned about my gifting. There are many people far more gifted than me. I couldn't keep up with them even if I tried. The Lord taught me through my mom and dad to simply be available to Him. This does not mean being available for service only, but staying in tune with Jesus, taking on His yoke and keeping in step with Him. Walking with Him, I have wound up in some unlikely places in this world. Being available to Him has always put me in the right places at the right times.

When we were living in Ethiopia, I needed to drive for long stretches between our mission station and Addis Ababa, where our children were attending our mission's boarding school. Planning to take a short break to go fishing one time, I felt a gentle nudge from the Lord not to do so. This Scripture came to mind, *"The mind of man plans his way, but the LORD directs his steps."*[2] "Okay Lord, I won't go fishing," I told Him. "Maybe there is someone else You are wanting me to talk with."

Further along the way I picked up a hitchhiker, a Jewish man who was camping his way through Africa. I had my camping gear with me, so we set up camp together. I thought about the story of Philip leading the Ethiopian to Jesus. Now here was I, an American camping with a Jew in Ethiopia. As we talked beside the campfire, I learned that he was born in America but had immigrated to Israel where he had been living on a Kibbutz. He said he was on a spiritual pilgrimage. This gave me a chance to tell him about my own spiritual story. I didn't consider myself an evangelist, but I knew I was in the right place at the right time. I explained the gospel to him and God opened his eyes to recognize that Jesus is the Messiah he had been waiting for. I was just available to point him to the One who was seeking him.

Now at the end of my life and service to Him, God has put me in another place – a hospital cancer ward. As in Ethiopia, Liberia and Russia, I want to be as available to Him here as I was there. He has led me here and He will walk with me through this valley. Once again, He has me in the right place at the right time. It's the story of my life.

2
Fanatical Faith of My Father

My parents, Arthur and Margaret Corey, were first-generation believers in Jesus Christ. First-generation Christians often have to plow through hard spiritual soil in a family line. There are sin-hardened attitudes and habits in every family, and the sins of our fathers can worm their way into several generations. Like immigrants in a new land, it is their children and grandchildren who benefit the most from the spiritual breakthrough that first generation believers have made in following after Christ.

Margaret and Arthur Corey

It was definitely tough spiritual tilling for my father.

He grew up in a Tacoma, Washington neighborhood, where all in the family were totally devoted to their respective professions. His parents were highly esteemed in their community and my grandfather held a respectable political office there. They held themselves and others to very high standards. They were moralistic people who attended a Presbyterian church about once a year, probably on Easter. Because they attended a very traditional church that placed a lot of emphasis on social life, it was a low blow to them when my father was wonderfully converted to Christ when he was a young man. They couldn't figure him out and they couldn't keep him quiet about his faith, so they labeled him a "fanatic" and ostracized him from the family. I don't have much recollection of them because I saw my grandparents only once or twice.

I recall my father's lively faith and sincere devotion to Christ. He and my mother left a spiritual legacy that is still bearing fruit to the glory of God through four successive generations in our family and even around the world. I am thankful for the spiritual foundation they gave to me. I have tried to do the same for my children and grandchildren.

In some ways my grandparents were right about my father; he was a fanatic, but in a solid biblical way. He was in his late twenties when he came to Christ in a camp meeting. A powerful evangelist had come to town and Dad went to hear him. He fell under conviction of sin and responded to the call to come forward and surrender his heart to Christ. He found a love in Him that he hadn't found in the traditional or social-minded church. It was a love that would change the course of his life, and it was a love that would change the course of his entire family line.

It was characteristic of my father to go all-out when he made up his mind to do something. After he had put his hand to the plow, he never again looked back. He was willing to pay the price of following hard after Christ.

At the time of his conversion, my parents were married with two kids. Dad had a good job, driving for a big trucking company. True to form, he quickly worked his way up the line to being the top driver in the company. Then the Teamsters came in and demanded a vote for joining the union. Dad didn't like their arm-twisting or their ungodly premises. This was during the Great Depression when jobs were scarce. But he wouldn't kowtow to coercion, so he was fired.

My mom didn't accept Christ when Dad did, and she did not like that he was a fanatic about his love for Jesus. She even considered divorcing him. But Dad turned the love that he was experiencing in Christ into a display of unconditional love to Mom. He went out of his way to serve her in every way he could. Finally, after about six months, Mom told Dad, "You win. I need what you have." And she came to Christ with her whole heart surrendered to Him.

From the beginning of his life in Christ until the day he died, my dad had a simple pure faith in Jesus. He literally took God at His word, and He believed every word in the Bible. So when he lost his job, he simply trusted God to provide new work. After several months of a difficult job search, he got a job feeding chickens on a big farm outside Tacoma. Although he had been brought up in the professional world, Dad wasn't too proud to do menial work.

He had been sickly much of his life and his skin had a tendency to break out with boils. In time Dad came to believe that God would heal him if he fully sought the Lord for healing. For three days he fasted without food or water. As he prayed for healing he also prayed for strength to do the hard work required in his job. Finally, after three days he felt the witness of the Spirit that God had healed him. Sure enough, God had healed him, and the boils never returned.

At the time of his conversion, Dad was a heavy smoker, smoking at least two packs a day. God began convicting him that smoking was harmful to his body, which was now the temple of the Holy Spirit. It was also a bad testimony and a waste of the money that God was providing for him. So he made a commitment to quit smoking for God's glory. He destroyed a full carton of cigarettes that he had recently purchased, and he decided to put a New Testament in his pocket where he had previously carried his cigarettes. Every time his hand went into his pocket to get another smoke, he pulled out that pocket Bible and read a passage from it. He never smoked again.

A short while later God spoke to Dad on three consecutive days, "Why are you feeding chickens? Feed my sheep." That's when Dad realized that the Lord was calling him into ministry. He talked with my mom about it. By this time she was committed to serving God along with Dad, and so he asked her if she had faith for him to quit his job and go out to serve the Lord full-time. Mom told him she didn't have the faith, but she knew that he did, and she was willing to follow him in whatever God led him to do. So he gave notice to his boss that he was quitting. That very day Dad received a letter in the mail with ten dollars in it. It was the first gift he had ever received. That was a lot of money in those days. Dad took it as confirmation that the Lord would provide for him and his family.

Losing two jobs in order to follow Christ during the Depression, when he had a wife and now three kids to provide for, made no sense to Dad's parents. It only gave them more proof that he was definitely an irresponsible religious nut. Later in their lives, both his mom and dad came to a living faith in Christ, but that was much later.

Dad had no seminary or Bible school training. He was taught by the Spirit, which meant that he was a serious student of the Bible and a real doer of the Word. For instance, in his study of the Word he felt God leading him to obey the command to *"sell all that you possess... and follow me."*[3] So in agreement with Mom he sold their house and most of their possessions. What he couldn't sell, he gave away.

Dad tried working with a Presbyterian ministry for about a year, but that was too stifling for him. Independent-minded ministers don't work well under lots of restraints and controls. So he quit that job too. By then, my older brother, Dave, had come along. Four kids and a wife, and no job during the Great Depression – the Lord had him just where He wanted him. He was fully dependent on God, and that is where he stayed for the rest of his life.

A friend of Dad's told him about a logging community called Joyce, in Clallam County, Washington, which is located outside of Port Angeles. There was no church in Joyce at that time, so no one invited him to come there and minister. But he felt the Lord was telling him to go there and preach the gospel. So that's how I wound up being born in Port Angeles. It was July 25, 1940.

Dad soon found out that he was not welcome in Joyce. Some people were outspokenly against having a church there. They were antagonistic toward the gospel. But that didn't dissuade him. He started looking around for a house to buy. His biggest problem was that he didn't have enough money to buy a house. He found an old grange community hall that was going up for sale at auction. It was big enough for both a home and a meeting hall. By the day of the auction all he had was $25, but he showed up anyway. As it happened, he was the only person present, so he got the lot and the building for what he had in his pocket.

That is, he got *most* of the lot and building. Soon after he bought the place, a neighbor approached him saying he had given the grange an easement before the building had been built because its lot was too small to build on, so he had let them build on a slice of property on his side of the line. Now that the grange had been sold, he wanted the part of the building that stood on his side. I don't know if the man was maybe trying to force my dad's hand into selling it all to him, but apparently he didn't know who he was messing with. Dad didn't flinch or fuss. He politely told the man he could have his piece of the building, but that his saw wasn't big enough to cut the building. He invited the neighbor to bring his own saw and they would cut off that part of the building for him to have. The two of them worked together pulling the crosscut saw until they had cut off the offending portion. Upon Dad's request, the neighbor let Dad use enough of the lumber to close up the open end of the building so we could move into our new home.

Dad started a little church in our home. There were only a few believers in the area, and I understand that some were pretty hardheaded. I can faintly remember some meetings going on there, but it eventually fell apart. My dad could also be pretty determined, so I think it was a mutual parting of the ways.

I was only about five years old when Dad decided we needed a bigger place. By then we had seven kids and we had outgrown the grange hall. It was situated on a pretty small lot, and Dad and Mom wanted space to grow a garden and build a larger home. But again, Dad had very little money. He had no regular paying job and he wasn't associated with any Christian organization. While he wasn't in the least lazy and was actually a hard worker, he knew that God had called him to work in His harvest field. Since He is the Lord of the harvest, that made Him Dad's boss. So he just looked to the Lord to provide our needs. And God's provision always came on time – sometimes just in time, but always on time.

There was a time when, for three days, all there was in the cupboard to feed us was beans. One night my mother prayed, "Lord, give us our daily bread." The next morning there were three loaves of bread on the table. Nobody knew where they had come from. In those days nobody locked their doors. My mother had recalled hearing some noise downstairs during the night, so apparently someone had come into the house and placed the bread there.

Just as we were enjoying our breakfast of fresh-baked bread that morning, a woman drove up to our home and knocked at our door. She said to Dad, "Mr. Corey, you probably don't know me, but yesterday while I was baking bread and then later when I went to bed, all I could think of was, 'Corey, bread. Corey, bread.' So I brought over those loaves and put them on your table. I also have a sack of flour in my car. If you can use it, you are welcome to have it."

Time and time again my parents saw God answering their prayers. So it wasn't too much of a stretch for Dad to believe that

God would also provide them with a better house and more property.

There was a 22-acre piece of wooded property about a quarter mile up the road. Dad would sometimes walk past it. He felt led to ask the Lord to give it to him. As he prayed about it, he grew confident that this would happen, so he approached the elderly lady who owned it and asked her how much she would sell it to him for. She said she wasn't interested in selling it; in fact, she said she planned to build on it herself. So Dad shook his head and said, "Lord, did I hear you correctly?" Then he just committed the whole matter to Him and left it alone.

In the meantime, a friend of my father's asked him to teach him about the life of faith. I was only five years old at the time, so I can't recall any details of the story, but this is how it went according to what I do know: They prayed and determined that the Lord was telling them to take a cross-country trip together, witnessing for Christ along the way, but they didn't know which way or how far the Lord would be taking them. My Dad added another stipulation. He insisted that they shouldn't take an extra purse or coat on the journey, just the clothes on their backs. This is the same stipulation the Lord gave when he sent out the seventy, and Dad took it as a personal directive. He didn't own a car, and probably the other man didn't either. So they needed to depend on the Lord to direct them and to provide their transportation. Keep in mind that this was all happening when there were seven kids still at home.

Off they went, without knowing where they were going. They walked along the road and took advantage of kind drivers who would stop and pick them up. They often walked for long stretches between rides. They ministered to many people along the way and eventually wound up in Kentucky before returning home, filled with praise to God for the great things He had done through them. The whole trip took six weeks. From some locations on their journey, Dad wrote notes to the family and sent home donations that people had given to him.

Shortly after his return, Dad learned that the lady who owned the property he had inquired about had died. He went to her son and daughter expressing his sympathy, and he informed them that he had inquired with their mother about the property. They were eager to sell it. He agreed to buy it for $1,000 with a $400 down payment followed by biannual payments of $50 plus interest, until it was paid off. Dad received the $400 necessary for the down payment on the agreed date at the end of 1945. Six months later, in June, he had made a one-time payment of $68. About that time my Uncle Emil and Aunt Hazel had felt the call to sell their place near Tacoma and go on staff at Prairie Bible Institute in Alberta, Canada. Uncle Emil was a superb machinist. He and Aunt Hazel came to help with the construction of our new home. He asked Dad how much he still owed on the property. When Dad told him $600, Uncle Emil took out six crisp $100 bills and handed them to Dad. He told him that was exactly the amount he had in mind to give as the tithe from selling his property.

These are the kinds of things that happened in the faith-filled atmosphere in which I grew up. I saw first-hand the faith of my parents and I saw God honoring their faith. Dad was not perfect. He was sometimes over-zealous and a little extreme in his doctrinal stands. But he was authentic and fully sincere in practicing what he believed. I learned from his example that faith is actually a very practical way of living. *"Show me your faith without the works, and I will show you my faith by my works,"*[4] wrote James.

My parents were hard-working people, and their faith showed up in their work habits. For instance, after the new property had been purchased, Dad didn't have money to buy materials for building a new home, so he dismantled the old grange house and he and my older siblings carried the lumber, board-by-board, a quarter mile up the road. I was too young to help and so I was sent to stay with my Aunt Hazel and Uncle Emil for most of the summer. I was not there to see it happening, but I was told that the family lined up like a colony of ants and carried pieces of lumber the quarter mile up the road. After awhile a couple of neighbors felt pity on the Coreys and they volunteered to haul several loads with their trucks. I suppose that provision was also a sign of the Lord's pleasure in my father's simple faith.

Dad built a tall, narrow barn-shaped house on the property using all that scrap lumber. He removed and straightened nails from the lumber as he dismantled the grange building. He reused those nails as he built our new home. Our house was really just a shell. It had no insulation. The studs were exposed on the inside and it was covered with shiplap and shingles on the outside. It had only a few small single-pane windows and so it didn't have a lot of natural lighting. During our first six months living there, we had no electricity and no running water, except when we kids went running down to the creek to fetch a pail of water.

New house built from the grange hall lumber

After we finally got electricity, Dad hooked up a pump that pumped water from the creek up to the house. I lived in that house from age six until I graduated from high school, and we never had an indoor toilet. There was a wood cook stove in the kitchen and a big pot-belly stove in the living room which heated part of the house. In winter, with wind blowing through the cracks in the wall, it could get cold enough in my little sleeping space under the roof on the second floor to freeze water. Thankfully we had lots of timber on the property to cut for firewood. My brother and sisters and I cut a lot of firewood after school and during the summer using an old crosscut saw and an axe.

That small house was not intended to be our permanent dwelling place. We eventually started building a bigger house on the property, which wasn't completed until I went off to Bible college.

Dad was as much a pragmatist as he was a man of faith. He was always building something and constantly trusting the Lord to guide and provide. And he had a King James Bible verse for every move he made. His verse for the new house was from Proverbs 24: 27 – *"Prepare thy work without, and make it fit for thyself in the field; and afterwards build thine house."*[5] It was largely my father's faith and service that prepared and fitted me for building a life of faith and service of my own.

3
Punching A Girl

Even when he was working, Dad was often mulling over Scripture. He so trained his mind in the Word that, even when he smashed his thumb with a hammer, his immediate response was to quote Scripture or to utter a prayer. I heard other men swearing when they smashed their thumb, but Dad didn't swear; he thanked the Lord. The measure of Dad's great faith was found in his response to the little tests he faced as much as it was in his big challenges.

I was deeply challenged one time when our cow was sick after giving birth to her calf. I remember Dad praying for three days that God would restore the cow. But on the third day when the cow didn't come to the barn, my brother Phil and I went looking for her. We found her dead under a tree up on a hill. When we came to Dad and reported that the cow had died, his first response was, "Thank you, Jesus." I simply could not understand that. Why would he thank the Lord for the cow dying when he had been praying that it would live? Besides, with such a large family, the milk from the cow was a valuable necessity. It wasn't until many years later that I learned for myself the real significance and release that comes from worshiping in the midst of trials.

When I was two years old I came down with whooping cough, pneumonia, and the measles, all at the same time. I was so sick I couldn't eat for days, and I was getting close to death. While my mother was constantly watching over me, my dad was praying, and he kept praying for me until he got assurance from the Lord that I was in His hands. So one evening Dad announced that he had a meeting to go out to and that my mom needed to go with him. He felt that she needed to release me to the Lord's care. At first she hesitated, but amazingly, as soon as she went with him, I started to get better and I was able to take in food. I soon recovered and was back to being a normal, rambunctious two-year-old.

Apparently I was still rambunctious when I was ten years old. One day a group of us kids were making lead fishing weights, pouring molten lead into wooden molds. I tossed some water on the hot lead to cool it down faster, which was a stupid thing to do. The lead exploded into my eyes. I was screaming in pain when my dad caught hold of me. He just held me and prayed. Then he took me to a doctor to get the lead plucked from my eyes. Looking at the burn damage, the doctor said he couldn't guarantee I would see again. He put patches over my eyes. A week later the doctor took off the bandages and was amazed at how well I had healed. He pronounced my eyes perfect. For years, Dad liked to boast in the Lord that I was the only one in the family who had never needed to wear corrective eyeglasses. But the Lord had much more to teach me before I was ready to follow Him wherever He would lead.

Interestingly, 40 years later the Lord would restore my daughter Debbie's eye as well, after a puncture from a scotch broom bush. My dad and I together would also have the same privilege to pray for her sight to be regained. By God's perfect plan and grace, she too was restored to full vision, much to the doctor's amazement, clearing us to return to the mission field and continue our work in Liberia.

As a kid, I constantly required lots of behavioral correction. I had a volatile temper. I don't know where I picked it up, except

22

from my sinful nature. My father didn't have a bad temper. In fact, if he did something wrong, he'd readily admit to it and quickly apologize. My mother certainly didn't blow up. But I did. If anyone crossed me, I would fight. I used to really get mad at my younger brother, Phil. I'd chase him and throw rocks and sticks at him. My parents were very concerned about me. I had many long walks to the woodshed with my dad for a time of close father-son, should I say, communication.

I am second on the left with seven siblings and my mother.

One day when I was about seven, two of my sisters were sawing wood and I asked them, "How can you know if you are saved?" Marilyn responded, "Well, have you asked Jesus into your heart?" I told her I had already done that. She said, "Well then, you are saved." But I didn't feel saved. I didn't behave saved either. It just kept gnawing at me. I hoped that maybe I could get into heaven because my parents were such good Christians, even though my folks had made it clear to me that it doesn't work like that. It had to be my own personal decision to accept Christ as

Savior. I definitely didn't want to go to hell, but I wasn't confident about my future in heaven either.

I went to a Bible camp when I was ten or eleven, and I remember going forward in a meeting to receive Christ again, just in case my previous decisions weren't sincere enough to get me into heaven. But my anger kept me feeling beaten and defeated, not saved, well into high school.

We didn't go to church as a family. We had church in our home. Every morning at breakfast we had ten or fifteen minute devotions. If Dad wasn't home to lead it, then Mom would. And if both of them were gone, one of my older sisters would read from the Scriptures and pray. Then on Sundays we gathered together and Dad would have a message for us from the Word. But his messages weren't limited to Sundays. He quoted the Scripture in everyday conversations. He was so full of the Bible, it just spilled out of him almost every time he opened his mouth.

Dad never tried to start another church. He met with a number of people in the area, teaching them from the Word in their homes. He just went wherever the Lord told him to go and he met with whomever He had arranged for him to meet. He was sometimes gone on trips for two or three weeks, as far away as Montana or Wyoming. Mom accompanied him on some of his shorter trips. They both were available to help anyone who needed prayer and encouragement from the Word.

My parents were big-hearted people. They brought a steady stream of troubled kids into our home. I've lost count of how many kids stayed with us over the years. Some of them were from the welfare system, which I suppose added a little income to the household. But some of the kids just needed a place to live. So they came and stayed for up to a year or several years. We were already crowded, but we always managed to make room for one more kid.

One boy who lived with us when I was in high school was mentally slow. He was probably fifteen. His parents weren't emotionally stable enough to care for him, so my folks said they would take him in. They were kind to him. At school, he was always the brunt of kids' jokes. Everybody else picked on him. I felt sorry for him and was always standing up for him. He stayed in a little room in our attic, which was right above my sisters' room. He made a peep-hole in the floor. When my parents discovered it, they realized they couldn't keep him around anymore. Dad was inquiring about a boy's home where he could stay when he disappeared. We didn't know where he had gone. Three days later a fisherman found him hanging from a rope down by the creek. I think he had lost all hope of ever having a home again. It was the only place where he had ever found acceptance and a place of refuge.

Growing up, I never had many friends. I had one good friend in high school, but I only saw him at school. Another boy lived up the hill behind us. He started coming over to our house, but then our dog chased him and bit him. I had to beat the dog with a baseball bat to get him off. We had to shoot the dog because of that. That also ended the boy coming over to our house. We lived in a spread-out community, so it was hard to make connections with other kids, especially with all the chores we had to do around the place. So we mostly just kept to ourselves.

But I think the main reason I didn't make many friends was my anger. Kids in school picked up on this and some of them tried to set me off. It didn't take much doing either. But it actually bothered me that I was so touchy. All the kids at school knew that I was a Christian, and I knew I wasn't being a good witness for Christ if I got mad when someone provoked me, but I just didn't know how to control my temper.

I think a lot of my anger problem was rooted in my family background. Both of my parents grew up in families where they were always being pushed to reach very high standards. I doubt that my dad's parents ever affirmed him. After he accepted the Lord, I think Dad must have transferred his own high expectations into his relationship with God. He was eager to please the Lord in all that he did, so he could only accept the very best, both from himself and from us. His intentions were good, but I seldom felt like I measured up to his standards. I remember one day reading fifty pages from the Scriptures and telling my dad what I had done, thinking he would be glad about that. His only comment was, *"Well, are you going to obey it?"* I can't remember him ever complimenting me or my brothers and sisters. Consequently, nobody in our family ever complimented or even thanked anybody for what they did. If we said anything to each other, it was a critical remark. I don't know if that explains my anger, but it sure didn't help it.

As He often does, the Lord used an apparent failure in my life to give me eventual victory over my anger. When I was in ninth grade, I had a literature teacher – definitely an unbeliever – who was telling an obscure story from the Old Testament in class. I thought I had heard every story in the Bible, but I couldn't remember this one. Then the teacher turned to me and said, "John, you're a Christian. How does the story end?" I sat there stunned and speechless. I had no clue. I had to admit out loud, "I don't know this story." I felt humiliated. I purposed that day to know God's Word so well that I would never again be embarrassed like that. Even though my motives may have been more self-preserving than pure, God used that embarrassing moment to motivate me to seriously read His Word. Like my Dad, I began to fill my mind with Scripture. As this happened, the Lord indirectly used that discouraging remark Dad had made when I told him about my Bible reading, *"Well, are you going to obey it?"* It made me want to be not only a reader of the Word, but a doer also. I greatly respected my father, and I wanted to please him. By becoming a doer of the Word, I knew I would be pleasing both God and my father.

I quickly found a lot of Scriptures that related to anger and showed how to overcome it. For instance, Proverbs 15:1 says, *"A gentle answer turns away wrath, but a harsh word stirs up anger."*[6] Mom and Dad liked to quote that one. I didn't have to look long or far to find ways to apply this passage. But first I was in for more failure.

There were several guys in school who liked to pick on me. One guy in ninth grade started bugging me when I was shooting baskets in gym class. Every time I shot the ball, he would toss a ball up and knock my ball from its trajectory. He kept bugging me and pestering me. I told him to knock it off or I was going to hit him. But he kept doing it. Finally I exploded and I charged him. Fists were flying between us, and my brother Dave and the rest of the team had to separate us.

There was also a girl in the school who used to pester me. I think she might have actually liked me, but she didn't know how to show it. I kept telling her to knock it off, but she just kept bugging me. Finally, I told her if she didn't quit it, I was going to punch her. If she was trying to get my attention, she didn't get the kind of attention she was hoping to get. I punched her. I didn't seriously hurt her, but I did seriously hurt my reputation. I had actually hit a girl, and nobody would let me forget it. It was like I was some kind of maniac. Some kids speculated that I might be facing criminal charges. In a small school, news like that didn't die down very fast. So not only was my Christian testimony suffering all the more, but I also got a reputation for being a girl-beater.

That was my last fight for a long time. I really regretted hitting that girl, and I told the Lord I was sorry. I asked His forgiveness. I knew He had died for me, but I still didn't know much about the Holy Spirit's control. Due to my frequent failures, I even questioned my own salvation. I still had a lot to learn about the greatness of God's grace, and I was still learning how to become a "doer of the Word." God used my antagonists to teach me, but I was also learning that the Holy Spirit is a much kinder and better teacher than my personal failures.

When I was a junior in high school, three freshmen started harassing me. Bill and Jack were cousins and Ronnie was their sidekick. They seemed to think their calling in life was to pester me. If we were riding on the school bus, that threesome would sit in the back and shoot spit wads at me. In the locker room they'd run by me and spill my books from a bench onto the floor. They did whatever they could to bug me. But God was working on me, and I was determined not to let them get the better of me. My brother Phil told me he would beat the tar out of them if they did all that to him, but I told him I had been doing that all my life. I wanted to change, which was a sign in itself that God was changing me.

We all had lockers assigned to us in the school hallway, but nobody ever locked them. One day a kid came into my class and said, "Hey, John, your stuff's scattered all over the hall."

I went out of the classroom and I could see my books, my jacket and my papers, everything spread clear down the hall. I gathered it all up and a friend offered to loan me his padlock. So now I was the only kid in school who locked his locker. Then one of them stuffed a matchstick up inside the keyhole so the janitor had to use a torch to burn it out. That ruined the lock so I had to buy my friend a new one.

The harassment continued off and on for about a year and a half. I never even uttered a word to those boys. I ignored every taunt they made at me. I didn't want to react negatively, so I didn't say anything at all.

A few months into my senior year, I was still locking my locker. Things had been rather quiet for a time without much harassment from the three guys, and so one day I decided to leave my locker unlocked and see what would happen. Sure enough, about five minutes later somebody said to me, "John, come see what's happened to your stuff!"

They'd taken everything out of my locker and spread it out the whole length of the hallway. I stood there looking over the damage. The three of them were standing down the hall, waiting for my

Senior in high school in Joyce, Washington

reaction. I was seething and I could feel my blood boiling. I walked up to them and jumped on Jack, the smallest of the three, and the others jumped on top of me. Phil started pulling them off of me. Teachers came running into the hall and broke it up. We were trotted away to the principal's office. Mr. Kratkey's first response to me was, "John, I thought you were a Christian. What are you doing in a fight?"

So I said, "Let me tell you a story." I told him about all that I had endured from those three guys over a year and a half without uttering so much as a word to them. But finally I'd had enough of it. The principal asked them if my story was true and they had to admit it was. So then he said, "Let's just put a stop to it and forgive one another." I said I was willing to do that. So we all agreed to forgive and forget. I never became real close friends with those boys, but we did become friendly. I talked with them occasionally, and they totally stopped bugging me. I look back on that as one of the most important growing times of my life. God was teaching me how to patiently endure trials, and when I read His instruction from the Word concerning anger, I was learning just what to do about it. *"A gentle answer turns away wrath, but a harsh word stirs up anger."[7]*

4
My Girl

Growing up on our wooded property, I learned to work with my hands. Most of our tools and equipment were old and worn-out. We had a rundown sawmill that someone had given to us. It was always breaking down, and we spent more time fixing it than actually running it. But we made the most of what we had. In some ways, working on that old contraption was a good life lesson for me. I can now see that God has used everything in my life – even my useless sins and mistakes – to make me more like Himself and to help me realize how dependent I am on Him and His grace.

As early as I can remember, my mother was praying that one of her children would serve the Lord as a missionary to Africa. He more than answered her request. Out of ten of us, six served in missions, I as a missionary to Africa and the other five elsewhere around the world. I don't know exactly when or how I knew that He was calling me to be a missionary. When I was in fifth or sixth grade I somehow knew that God had His hand on me. I couldn't have told you why I knew it. I didn't even know the Scriptures well enough to know how God calls people to serve Him. It was just an awareness I had that He had set me apart to be a missionary.

Like that old sawmill, the Lord put more into preparing me to serve Him, even after I was on the mission field, than the service

He actually ever got out of me. If I have been of any use to Him, it's only by His grace.

I never was much for studying in school. Math and science came easy to me, but I didn't like to read and I was horrible at writing. Maybe I could have gone on to become an engineer or some other mathematical profession like that, but to me that seemed about as dry as eating sawdust. I knew God was calling me to be a missionary, and that meant I would need to somehow learn to study. So I looked into a few Bible schools. I wrote to Columbia Bible College and to Multnomah School of the Bible and also to Prairie Bible Institute in Canada.

I kept praying and asking God to show me where to go. My brother Dave was going to Seattle Pacific and he kept telling me to go there. He said there were plenty of Bible classes I could take there. But I didn't want to just study the Bible. I wanted to go somewhere that would prepare me for missions. I kept wrestling in prayer, and the more I struggled and prayed, the stronger I felt about God's call on my life. One day while I was having my devotions, I heard the Lord tell me, "Prairie. Go to Prairie."

Once again, I can't explain how I knew it was Him. It wasn't an audible voice. But it was perfectly clear to me that the Lord had spoken to me. It was a very definite sense in my soul. So I called my brother and announced with no hesitation, "I'm going to Prairie."

The next thing I did was fill out an application. I sent it in, but before I had even received acceptance I packed up and left for Prairie Bible Institute in Three Hills, Alberta, Canada. I got there before they had even processed my application. But that presented no problem to me. I had no question about my being there. If they hadn't yet completed the process, that was their problem. I was ready to enroll. I felt the Lord had been preparing me for this my entire life. Needless to say, they accepted me. They had to, because God had sent me there. I was convinced of it. The only question I had was for how long.

I was sure of my calling, but I wasn't too sure of myself as a student and I didn't know if I could make it through the school year. I figured I'd just try to make it through that first year. But after meeting some of the other students, I was sure I wanted to go there all four years. I had never had any true spiritual fellowship with anyone in high school. Then all of a sudden I was talking with other guys who had genuine hearts for God. It felt like I was in heaven. The first week I was there I wrote to my mother and told her I was going to stay at Prairie for the full four years. I might not have been much of a student, but I did love the Lord and His Word, and I couldn't get enough of either.

I had a gradual "grace-dawning" while I was at Prairie. I was pretty legalistic when I first got there, having lived under my father's influence and never feeling like I could measure up to his high standards. I didn't yet have a clear understanding of the freedom we have in Christ. I felt called to be a missionary and was willing to go anywhere to serve Him, but I didn't yet know how to walk with Him to get there.

There were some terrific Bible teachers at Prairie, most notably L.E. Maxwell, the founder of the school. He wrote a book, *Born Crucified*, which spells out our true identity in Christ. It explained how we were bought with the blood of Jesus and how we were co-crucified with Him on the cross. Since we don't belong to ourselves, it is our responsibility to surrender to His lordship over our lives.

That's the kind of teaching that pervaded the atmosphere at Prairie. I began to learn what grace is really about. It didn't come to me through a single source. It was all around me. Through my studies, I was getting immersed in the Word of God. The Bible instructors were excellent and some powerful speakers came and spoke during chapel services. I also engaged in deep spiritual discussions with my peers.

I spent a lot of time alone, praying and striving to understand the meaning of scriptures. My first-year roommate in the dorm didn't show up, so I had plenty of time for that. I had always been a loner anyway, so it didn't bother me. During my junior year I was appointed Residence Assistant, which meant I had a room to myself. So I had no real distractions in my pursuit of knowing God.

I didn't want to merely know right doctrine. I was absolutely serious about knowing the Lord Himself through His Word.

At that time, Prairie was known for its rigid rules. It probably wasn't entirely unlike other Bible schools in those days, but you had to toe the line around there. Some guys were always bucking the system. Not me. My life was already in line with any of the restrictions the school had laid out for students. The tightest constraint had to do with male and female associations. Engagements among students were forbidden. No unsupervised contact was allowed between males and females. Men and women sat on separate sides of the dining room. You couldn't even speak with the opposite sex. You couldn't write a letter. During off hours from school, guys and gals couldn't go into town at the same time. If the men went west, the women had to go east. My sister Eleanor came to Prairie when I was a junior. I could only visit with her once a month. But none of that bothered me a bit. I wasn't interested in getting involved with any girl anyway. I was totally focused on heeding God's call to the mission field. And besides, I was always struggling with my class assignments. I didn't have time for anything but studying.

During the summer between my junior and senior year, my brother Dave asked me, "John, how are you ever going to find a wife if you don't date?" I'd never had a date in my life and I had no interest in finding a wife. I told him, "I know what God has called me to do, and when He brings the right one along, I know I won't miss her."

I thought that sounded pretty good. I could think of only one criterion I wanted in a wife: she had to be called to missions. But there was one young lady who had made a distinct impression on me. During my junior year I was waiting on tables during the mission conference. A girl was sitting with her mother whose hair was snow white. It really stood out so I couldn't help but notice her. But I also noticed her daughter and I felt something inside me say, "This is nice." It was the first time I had noticed Jeanette, and it was the first time I had ever felt something like that.

During the summer I worked at Lake Sammamish Bible Camp (Sambica) near Seattle. Jeanette was also working there as a camp counselor. I arrived later than her. Somehow she knew I would be working there that summer, so when I didn't show up, she started wondering where I could be. We had already made some kind of an impression on each other. Jeanette was working at the information booth, so I'd stroll by and we'd talk. She was very shy, but I had no problem talking with her. We discovered we had a lot in common. She also felt called to missions, and more specifically she felt the Lord was directing her to Ethiopia, where, by then, I sensed the Lord was calling me to go.

I'll need to backtrack here to explain how all that got started. During my first year at Prairie I voluntarily started attending daily missions' prayer meetings for different continents. I felt most comfortable praying for Africa. At least half of the prayer letters we prayed through came from missionaries attached to SIM. I got very interested in working with SIM. All the while I kept praying, "Lord, where do you want me to go?"

One day a SIM missionary named Hedley Waldock spoke in chapel. He was serving in Ethiopia. As he was telling about the people there, I felt really drawn to go there too. I sensed that God was saying, "I want you in Ethiopia."

Hedley's wife was from Emmanuel Bible Church in Seattle, the same church that Jeanette had grown up in. Her parents were friends with the Waldocks and often had them in their home for a meal. Jeanette felt drawn to Ethiopia by listening to the Waldocks tell their stories.

So when Jeanette and I met and started swapping stories, we discovered we shared the same heart burden for Ethiopia and we'd been influenced to go there by the same couple. The more we talked at the information booth that summer at Sambica, the more we seemed to click. Then I got to wondering, "Is this the one I told my brother I wasn't going to miss?"

Early that summer my friend Dan asked me to go out on a double-date with him and his lady friend. I told him I wasn't interested. But as the summer went on and I got to know

Jeanette, it started to seem like a pretty good idea. I was feeling strongly attracted to her. She had a genuine, quiet humility that I really liked. I could see she was also very serious about her studies. I had never met a girl who held such an appeal. I guess there's some kind of a chemical reaction that happens when a guy meets a certain girl. Whatever it was, it was happening to me over her. So I asked my friend if he still wanted to go out on a double-date. A couple we knew was getting married, so that seemed like the perfect occasion to ask Jeanette to go along with me.

Jeanette later told me she couldn't sleep all night after I had asked her to go out with me. So I guess the chemical reaction was going on in her too. Anyway, I don't remember a lot about the wedding, but I do remember what it was like to be out with her. It sort of sealed the deal in my mind. I was already convinced she was the kind of girl I was waiting for. I was eager to get to know her better, so I found as many ways to spend time with her as I could.

For the rest of the summer we went on walks together during our free time. The more time I spent with her, the more eager I was to be with her once again. But then I started to worry that, now that we were spending time together, would I be able to pull back if it wasn't God's will for us to marry? I had never felt this way about a girl, so I was fearful about my feelings toward her. I started asking all kinds of questions that I could not answer. For instance, I wondered what would happen if we went to Ethiopia and Jeanette got sick. Would we need to leave the mission field? I prayed a lot about this.

About a month into our relationship, I went to the lady who ran the camp, Aunt Ruby. She was a godly woman who had a gentle, wise spirit. I told her about my struggles concerning Jeanette and my call to Ethiopia. I told her my worries about the future. Aunt Ruby's counsel was clear and simple: "You can't know tomorrow." Then she directed me to Isaiah 32:17, *"The work of righteousness shall be peace; and the effect of righteousness quietness and assurance for ever."*[8]

That verse hit my heart, and it's been a life verse for me ever since. Aunt Ruby explained that if God was in our relationship, then there would be peace. He doesn't expect me to know the future. That's His realm, not mine. That helped me to relax and enjoy the moment. And when I let go of my worries, the peace of the Lord flooded my heart. I knew it was right to go forward with Jeanette.

When we returned to Prairie that fall, I had to make every move count in order to see Jeanette. Due to the no-contact policy, my timing needed to be perfect. Jeanette sang in the school choir and at the same time I practiced in the orchestra in another building. During the next hour we both had accordion lessons in separate rooms of that building. So I would position myself in the men's latrine and watch through a window for her to pass by. When she came my way, I'd fall in line about two or three steps behind her and we'd climb up the stairway together, going to our separate classes, perfectly paced and perfectly spaced. That way we wouldn't get called in for violating the no-contact rule. I don't think Jeanette ever knew about my strategy. I kept it a secret from her so she could truly be innocent in case she was ever questioned. It was just nice to see her every day, and I suppose she didn't feel too badly about seeing me either.

Like I said, I didn't have any problems with the rules at Prairie, but I had to learn to be creative with them. Apparently others also learned to creatively work within the rules, because there were ten or twelve other couples who announced their marriage engagements after our class graduation that year.

You couldn't get engaged while studying at Prairie, but if there was an "understanding" between a guy and a girl during their fourth year there, they could arrange for monthly appointments to see each other in the ladies dean's office. The meetings took place behind a curtain in her office. You could sit with plenty of space between you on a couch and talk softly to each other. The dean was elderly and hard-of-hearing, so I don't think she could listen in, but just in case, you always had to keep your voices down and not get too excited over anything.

So one day when Jeanette and I were meeting behind the curtain, I just kind of out-of-the-blue asked her to marry me. Actually, I knew all along that I wanted to marry her, but suddenly I just couldn't stop myself from asking her, so I just popped the question. When she said yes, I kissed her. Right there in the dean's office, behind the curtain. I kissed her!

Well, of course we had to keep it a secret until after graduation; otherwise we'd have been kicked out of school. During the summer we worked together again at Sambica and we made an official announcement of our engagement on July 25th, my birthday.

Jeanette and I had both applied to go to Biola School of Missionary Medicine in Los Angeles, thinking that training would be of practical use on the mission field. It started on September 1st and we figured it would be better for us to be married than to live separately as students. We set a wedding date for August 25th 1962, and Jeanette quit the camp to work on preparations. A month's engagement was rushed. It would have been better for us to be officially engaged earlier in the summer so Jeanette would have had more time. Her parents wanted us to wait until Christmas. But we didn't do it that way. We did it my way. I started dominating the major decisions in the wedding and I put a lot of pressure on Jeanette before the wedding instead of hearing her out as I should have done.

Marrying the girl I couldn't miss

Jeanette isn't the kind to speak up about what she is really feeling, and I just didn't ask her to find out. Years later she told me my choice of honeymoon spots – camping in the Olympic Forest – wouldn't have been her first choice. But she realized I didn't have any money and thankfully she was adventuresome enough to go along with it. But we did share our deep love for the Lord. For the wedding ceremony we borrowed a large plaque that read, *"O magnify the Lord with me, and let us exalt His name together."*[9] We both loved that verse and we thought it would be a good motto for our life together. And it has been. I will have it inscribed on my tombstone and so will Jeanette.

I think there's a lot of truth in the biblical principle of not going out to war for a year after you marry. The first year of our marriage, while we were studying at Biola, was pretty intense. We lived in a cramped, 12' by 12' room. The demands of our studies kept us under constant pressure. I always had to study harder than anybody else just to make C's. I rarely made a B, and I never made A's. I wasn't a good student, but I was a serious student. Jeanette was a much better student than me. I sometimes would get uptight and upset with myself. Then my emotions would boil over on Jeanette.

She grew up in a home where no one ever argued or raised their voices. She had just one sister, Irene, whose temperament is about the same as hers. Her Swedish parents were quiet, solid

Jeanette and her younger sister, Irene

38

people who loved the Lord, and love always filled their home. They were very supportive of one another, always building each other up and never tearing down.

My parents were both godly, but because of the high standards my father had for himself, we all had the same standards put on us. We never compli- mented each other. We were always competing with and criticizing each other. We'd argue and yell and not even think twice about it. Jeanette had never been hollered at.

I don't remember what our first argument was about, but I do remember

Waldie and Esther Hawkinson, Jeanette's parents

that I lost. I got angry about some little thing and I raised my voice at Jeanette. It was the first time I had ever heard a woman crying over an argument. What do you do with a crying wife? I had no idea what to do. So I had to walk out and cool down.

It happened like that fairly often. Afterwards I would apologize and ask her to forgive me. She was kind and tenderhearted and she would forgive me. But it was a big learning curve for me. After all the teaching I had received at Prairie about the "surrendered life," the Lord was using my young wife to teach me how to surrender in ways I hadn't realized I would need to know.

As time went on, I made a commitment to Jeanette to never publicly speak negatively of her, neither to our children nor to anyone else. As far as others knew, I have had a perfect wife. She certainly has been the perfect wife for me. Jeanette has a real merciful heart and she has been totally devoted to our family. I've made more mistakes than I can remember, but the Lord didn't let them go to waste. Like that old sawmill, He was always working on me and giving me grace so that I could be useful to Him.

5
Rough Waters

Sometimes determining God's leading hasn't been completely clear. With the benefit of hindsight, I can now see that going through the medical training at Biola during our first year of marriage was not the best plan, and it may not have been God's plan for Jeanette and me. He did use it to give me some important character lessons, but I'm sure He could have done that in other ways without it being so hard on us during our first year of marriage. We rarely used the medical training we got there, except for tending to family needs, because in Ethiopia we had a clinic and a nurse near us. It probably would have been better if I'd gotten a job during that first year or maybe if I had worked as an assistant pastor in a small church so I could have gained some ministry experience. I can now see the value of the biblical principle of "staying out of the battle" during the first year of marriage.

But at that time in my life it would have been awfully hard for me to change my course for any reason. I was absolutely determined to get out to the mission field, specifically to Ethiopia. Doing anything else might have seemed disobedient to me. So while we were studying at Biola, Jeanette and I were busy applying for SIM's Missionary Candidate School in Pasadena. We finished our medical training by the first of August and we were at the candidate school in November. By then Jeanette was expecting our first child, Melodie. She was born January 28, 1964. We waited about three months after her birth to begin our deputation, seeking financial and prayer support.

One of the first churches we went to was a small church in Oregon, near Portland. It was called Progress Bible Church. Our SIM regional director had a mission conference there and so Jeanette and I went down to Portland to participate. I don't think we picked up any financial support from there at that time, but we did gain some friends and more prayer support. Eventually that church became Southwest Bible Church in Beaverton, which is now our home church and one of our greatest sources of support and encouragement.

In those days we needed only $300 a month to be fully funded on the field in Ethiopia. Of course, that was still a lot for us to raise at that time, and most of it came to us through small monthly commitments of $10 or $20. But God supplied all of our needs and we started our journey to Ethiopia by train from Vancouver, British Columbia. My folks prayed and said farewell to us in Seattle and Jeanette's parents accompanied us to Vancouver.

Along the way, we marveled at the beauty of the Canadian Rockies. It was a pleasant journey until we got just past Winnipeg, when Melodie became seriously ill. She was running a high fever and vomiting with diarrhea. She became severely dehydrated and we were really worried by the time we arrived in New York City. We rushed her to a hospital and the pediatrician who saw her said we got there without a moment to spare. We almost lost her. They had to strap her on a bed and put her on IVs for two days. The Lord rescued Melodie, and we thanked Him for the excellent hospital staff who gave her such great care. She was soon running all around, full of energy.

In New York, we boarded a Norwegian freighter, the *Concordia Viking*, which took us all the way to Ethiopia. We departed in April of 1965. It was a six-week trip. There were ten other passengers aboard, all older people who were well-to-do

world travelers. It was a treat for them to see little Melodie running up and down the "hills" on the deck of the ship as it rose and fell with the ocean swells. The ship was safely fenced so we had no concern about her falling overboard. We were privileged to dine with the ship's captain and every meal was a real smorgasbord. On Jeanette's birthday, the captain and other passengers toasted her. She and I drank pop.

It was a fairly smooth trip that included some interesting stopping places. Across the Atlantic, we stopped in the Canary Islands. We also docked in Naples, Italy for a week and then went on to Florence and visited some missionary friends from Seattle.

Traveling by freighter for the first time to Ethiopia

We held a little church service on board the ship every Sunday and a Swiss stewardess accepted Christ as her personal Savior. She had an Italian Catholic religious background. At first she said it would cost too much for her to become a Christian, but I explained the gospel to her and quoted Jesus saying, "Behold, I stand at the door and knock. If anyone hears My voice and opens the door, I will come in to him."[10] It was amazing to see the light dawning on her face. She really understood what God had done for her. After she had prayed and received Christ, I gave her the promise of Jesus: "I will never leave you nor forsake you."[11] She was very happy to hear that. She had lost her husband eight months previously and had felt the loss deeply. After that, our new friend came to our stateroom nearly every day.

Before passing through the Suez Canal, we anchored offshore from Port Said, Egypt. By the time we had our passports processed, we only had about two hours to go ashore. In Port Said we were hounded left-and-right by sellers to buy all kinds of items. We said no to everything, except we bought a dozen small bananas for about eight cents.

We also anchored outside of Port Sudan for 72 hours. The heat there was stifling. A dark Sudanese man and his Egyptian wife and two children came aboard. Melodie was very interested in the color of their skin. By the time we arrived at the port of Massawa, the heat was almost unbearable. After taking a shower and getting dressed, we already felt the need for another shower. Fortunately we didn't stay there long. We boarded a bus that took us to higher ground in Asmara before going on to Addis Ababa, Ethiopia. We then went to Debre Berhan, which is located 9,000 feet above sea level. It got down into the cool 40's at night. It was so cold we needed sweaters. We had brought some sweaters along for the trip across the ocean, not realizing we would need them near the equator in Africa. We were very glad we had them when we discovered how cool it could get at that altitude.

The Ethiopian people are a beautiful people, with light-brown skin and fine features; they are often dressed in white garments. But there are also some gruesome sights among the populace. It was at first shocking to see lepers along the way, toes and fingers gnawed off by rats. Little kids had infected, oozing eyes with flies crawling over the goop on their faces. Blindness is common there, and its chief cause is the lack of hygiene. It seemed there were maimed and crippled people every place we went.

Cows and donkeys crowded the streets, and cars and trucks simply found a way around them. People would sometimes run wildly alongside a moving vehicle, darting into its path and jumping back, hoping a spirit that was haunting them would get run over. Sometimes the people would get struck and injured or killed by the vehicle. That's how desperate they were to find release from the spirits. When someone had died, we heard this horrible wailing that went on and on. It was the cry of people who really had no hope beyond the grave. But we had brought the message of hope with us to Ethiopia.

Our language school in Debre Berhan was a nine-month course. We started there in May of 1965, staying in a two-room flat. A lady named Wusunee came to us six days a week to care for Melodie. She wore beautiful flowered dresses and a tight-fitting head tie. She spoke no English and at first Melodie was scared of her. In the manner of Ethiopian women, however, Wusunee carried Melodie around on her back and Melodie soon came to adore her. We paid Wusunee $1.20 per week, which was the going rate for a nursemaid.

Melodie with Wusunee

Jeanette was pregnant with Reenie when we started language school, so learning a new language was tremendously challenging for her. The national language of Ethiopia is Amharic, after the tribe of Emperor Haile Selassie, who was the beneficent dictator at that time. Amharic is a very difficult language by any standard. It is 40 percent cognitive with Hebrew, comprised of 26 consonants that have seven different vowel sounds that alter the sound of the consonants depending on how they are drawn into the script. It meant we had to learn a whole new way of writing as well as speaking. We struggled day and night to learn our lessons. Just when we thought we were getting out from under one pile, our instructor would dump on us a load of new words, consonants, vowels and sayings to learn. But it was essential to learn the language before we could report to our assignment in the field. So despite my natural inability to learn a language, I was highly motivated to learn it anyway and get on with the reason we had come to Ethiopia.

Each day, six days a week, we listened for about two hours to taped recordings from our lessons. We practiced repeating everything we had heard in class. Then we practiced with an "informant" for another hour so that we could correct our pronunciation. After that, we went out into the community and rehearsed our lines with anyone who would listen. At first, we asked simple questions like, "What is your name?" and "How

Language practice with informant, laughing at ourselves

many children do you have?" The people were patient with us, but they probably cringed a little when they saw us coming day after day with new lines to practice.

Several months into our language school, the SIM mission board asked us to leave our studies and go to the missionary school, Bingham Academy, in Addis. They needed some dorm parents there and they thought Jeanette and I would be a good fit. It definitely would have been easier on Jeanette because she was carrying Reenie at the time and Melodie was a toddler. Being new to the country, we were constantly sick with stomach ailments, vomiting and dashing to the outhouse. But I just couldn't do it. I pleaded with them to let us stay and finish language school. I strongly felt my calling was to teach at a Bible school to develop church leaders. Learning the language was essential to that and I didn't want to be diverted.

Finally they found another couple to fill the need and we were allowed to finish our course. But it was still hard. Before finishing language school, we had to translate the Gospel of Mark into Amharic. It took hours to translate just one chapter. And then we had to pass the mid-term and final exams. It was really overwhelming. As I would later find out while teaching at the Bible school, my language-learning struggles helped me to better relate with the students there, because learning the Bible came just as hard to them as learning their language had come to me.

Reenie was born six weeks before we finished language school. That made it much more difficult for Jeanette to study. But she prayed as hard as she studied. Then Melodie came down with the measles and the mumps. And just before our final exams I got the mumps. I was really sick with a fever and had to stay in bed. Determined to finish the course, I studied and took the final exam in bed. It was a long and grueling test. Jeanette had to pause twice to feed Reenie. When she learned that she had passed the test, she cried tears of relief.

We soon learned that we had been assigned to a remote place called Burji. It was at a lower elevation (about 6,000 feet), so it would be warmer there. We took a little time off before we reported to our new home. Then Jeanette contracted malaria. It was one thing after another, but we knew we were called by God to be there. We kept thanking Him and He gave us the grace we needed to face each new challenge.

Traveling to Burji for our first assignment

6
Now You Understand Us

The mission work in Burji was started in about 1949 by an Australian SIM missionary named Alex Fellows. I don't know much about him personally, but I can say by the widespread fruit of his labor that he was mainly an evangelist. Over a 15-year period, about 70 to 75 churches had started in a broad area in the Amaro

Burji compound where we lived for over nine years

Mountains, which climb in a long ascent from the Rift Valley to about 11,000 feet above sea level. There are three main tribes living there – the Guji, a cattle-grazing nomadic people, the Quara and the Burji, which were agricultural tribes. The Lord used Alex Fellows to plant the churches, and it fell on me and other SIM missionaries to develop them.

To build churches, it is necessary to first build leaders, getting them established in the Bible. When we arrived in Burji, only a few leaders could read or write Amharic, and consequently they had very little firsthand knowledge of God's Word. This resulted in complete ignorance of God's grace in Christ and how He works in the lives of individuals and in the church. Some claimed that they had the Holy Spirit and therefore had no need of being taught in the Word. The effect of that thinking was a widespread and deeply entrenched spirit of legalism. A person was considered a Christian if he or she started coming to church and didn't drink and didn't wail at funerals. I was very grieved by the hardness I saw among the leaders toward their people. Trusting in Christ's death and resurrection had little or nothing to do with salvation, according to these legalists. Some of them started to understand the gospel, but they were slow to respond because they were stuck in the rules of religion rather than relying on the grace of God. All this confusion and vying for power was related to the people's ignorance of the Word.

The Ethiopian government required mission stations to establish schools and medical clinics as an entry for ministry. This actually worked out in our favor. When we arrived in Burji, there were approximately 150 children enrolled in the school on our compound. Our literacy training was very basic, but at least it was a first step forward in teaching them from God's Word.

Another big challenge was that the churches were so spread out, and transportation between them was extremely difficult. The road in the area was nothing more than a pathway covered with deep ruts and big boulders. The road ended at Burji; from there we had to walk, or go by mule or motorcycle. The Guji people were especially hard to reach because they were constantly following their cattle to greener grass. They were also hostile. To prove their manhood, it was required of a young Guji to kill a male Quara or Burji and bring a slice of his skin to the young lady in his life. The witch doctors also held a lot of sway over the people. They lived in constant fear of his power. And because they couldn't read the Word, they didn't realize the authority God had given them in Christ over demonic powers. These were just a few of the challenges we faced. But it kept us constantly praying for wisdom and grace to do the work the Lord had called us to among those people.

Our Bible school was also very basic. It had to be. The national language in Ethiopia is Amharic, but it is not the language of all the people. Each tribe has its own language. When I began teaching in the Bible School, I barely had a working knowledge of Amharic. So I was teaching in a strange language, and the students were trying to learn in a language that was also strange to them. I studied for many hours to develop a ten-minute lesson in Amharic. The best I could do was to then write out the entire lesson on a chalkboard, and the students would copy it and learn it by rote. This approach suited them anyway because in their culture a student never questions a teacher or an elder. It was good because they were listening, but it also made it hard to

Teaching in the Burji Bible School

teach on subjects such as God's grace and mercy, because these are truths that cannot be grasped by simply repeating a lesson word-for-word. I understood that only the Holy Spirit can lead a person to understand these truths, so I taught through Romans several times during my years there.

While I was teaching, I was also learning to teach. One of the greatest lessons I learned was that I was not just teaching scriptural subjects – I was teaching people. There's an important difference. I tried to make every lesson practical to their own lives. God's truth is not just academic. It is powerful to change lives.

Even when a student did begin to grasp the truth of the gospel, the legalistic elders at their churches usually refused to let him teach. They did not allow younger members to have a position of influence over them. So I encouraged the students to teach people one at a time; to make disciples. It didn't matter if they had a big following or not, only that they were following the Lord's command to make disciples, teaching them to obey all that Jesus had commanded them. I encouraged them to humbly serve the Lord and be faithful in the opportunities He put in front of them, trusting that He would lift them up in due time.

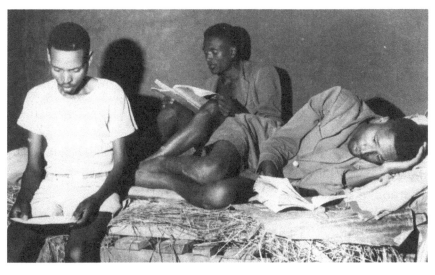

Bible school students studying on their stick beds

I appreciated the commitment and sacrifice it took for students to attend the Bible school. Some came from far-off villages, requiring a three or four-day journey. Most walked or jogged the whole way. They carried their own supplies of wheat in a cloth hanging from their walking sticks, and they slept on animal skins stretched over stick beds. They also paid for their own tuition by selling chickens or other tradable merchandise. We knew it would mean more to them if it cost them something. It was very little by our standards, but it was a lot to them.

The Bible school ended at two o'clock on Thursday afternoons each week. Most students made their way home and I often went out to one of the villages to help build a church building. I built many churches during my time there. The typical building was a mud hut with a thatched roof. A pole in the center of the building held the roof together. I made trusses that crossed the room, requiring no center pole, and attached a tin roof. That was quite a novelty to the people. They couldn't understand why the roof didn't cave in without a center pole.

Constructing a church building

At first I went all the way to the various villages on the back of a mule. That was a slow go. Eventually I got a Kawasaki motorcycle, which enabled me to climb way up the mountain to the remote villages. The Land Rover, which came later, turned out to be the only vehicle in the area, so I was constantly hauling materials and goods for all kinds of uses. The road was so rough and slippery in the rainy season that I drove with chains on all four wheels to make my way through the mud. Once, while trying to get over rocks and potholes, an axle broke. I overhauled or replaced almost every part on that Land Rover, including the engine and the transmission.

There was hardly a day that went by when I didn't use the mechanical know-how I had picked up on the farm where I grew up. It would have been impossible to make it out there in the bush without some practical skills. The Lord had me well-prepared for that kind of life. Back home, we were always figuring out ways to make things work. Even if we'd never tried it before, we just kept tinkering until the problem was solved.

In Burji there was no public electricity, but there was plenty of wind for making it. In the mornings, 25-mile-an-hour winds would rise up from the heat exchange coming from the Segen Valley below. A missionary family before us, the Edighers, had brought a wind-charger from the Midwest. It powered a 32-volt

Restructuring the wind charger

electric system for the compound, but it didn't catch the wind very well. So another missionary, Ben Smith, and I set it up at a higher location where it could really catch the wind. Sometimes there was too much wind. We made a 12-volt system on all the houses using car batteries and 12-volt light bulbs. That system could also pull 30 volts for doing some heavy welding. While on furlough, I later picked up some rechargeable batteries, which meant we didn't need to constantly replace worn-out batteries. I did have to rebuild some of the rechargeable batteries, but it was better than constantly hauling in big, heavy batteries. It was just one of those things I had to figure out how to do.

The house we first lived in had a sagging ceiling and a sloped floor. Alex Fellows had built it with the help of some Ethiopians. He had no experience in building. The walls were set directly on the ground and termites had chewed away on them. The floor buckled up in the middle and sagged along the walls, which were made of mud mixed with straw. It was like a house built on sand with no solid foundation. It had a kitchen, a dining room, a living room and two bedrooms. It served us for the time being. Later we moved into a better house. But neither house had an indoor bathroom. We had a wood stove for cooking. I ran a metal pipe through it for heating water. We had no running water except for the rain we caught in a barrel running off the roof. We also had an unreliable well.

Getting mail from home is like lifeblood for missionaries. This was especially so during those days before email and phone service. It had to come in by airplane. A Missionary Aviation Fellowship plane brought us mail every four to six weeks. That meant any letter we received would take that long again before we could send a response. It usually took about a three-month turnaround between a letter sent and a letter received from the States. But it was always worth the wait. Jeanette was faithful in writing family, supporters and prayer partners, often sending personal notes. Careful to not miss anyone, she kept charts on who needed to hear what about the happenings on the mission field. This was vital in helping others to understand what we were walking through.

Due to the strong winds, it was often tricky for the pilots to land on the airstrip we had near Burji. There was a windsock beside the strip that indicated which way the wind was blowing to help the pilot guide the plane down safely. But it wasn't always a sure sign of which way the wind was blowing. I remember one time the sock was flying straight up, which looked like it was hanging straight down to the pilot up above it. But the wind was actually rushing so hard upward from the valley that it had made a strong updraft. When the pilot tried to touch down the plane, it got thrown upward and he nearly crashed into the gully. But those pilots were very skilled and, after a few rounds, he finally made it to the ground. We praised the Lord for His protection.

Ben Smith and his family left Burji after they went on furlough, leaving us with a teacher and a nurse. It got pretty lonely at times, especially when our kids were old enough, at age six, to go away to Bingham Academy in Addis Ababa. Sending the kids to boarding school was something Jeanette and I knew we needed to do; we had agreed to do so even before we married. It was just part of the missionary life. It's what all missionaries did in those days, but that didn't make it any easier, especially on Jeanette.

After the kids went to school, she shed lots of tears. We were careful not to make it seem like a negative thing for our kids. We wanted them to see the privilege of going away to school, so we'd get them looking forward to the experience, saying things like, "When you *get* to go to school, you'll learn how to read and write and you'll have lots of friends." Jeanette was really good at helping the kids stay positive. She wrote letters every week to each child and sent packages of roasted wheat, homemade crackers and other treats whenever she could. She encouraged them to look for ways to help other kids who were having a hard time there. To this day, our kids still thank us for allowing them to go to boarding school. They made many good friends and received an education they could not have otherwise had in such a remote location.

Our kids also had many friends among the tribal kids. Kids have ways of understanding each other even when they don't speak the same languages. I remember Melodie coming inside and telling us a story about what the other kids on the compound were telling her. There were kids from the Burji, Quara, and Welayta tribes; some spoke Amharic, and then our kids spoke English. So there were five languages between them, and they were all telling one story. We asked them how they understood it all. They just looked at us and said, "We just do!"

But most of the national kids were soon so taken up by their responsibilities at home, caring for younger siblings and doing chores, they had little time for play. Their childhood was very short.

In fact, it was very common to lose a child in infancy. It was a grief that was a way of life for the people there. It was also a grief that we would soon share with them. Our son Nathan was born after we had come to Burji. He was a fun little guy, always curious and getting into things like all little boys do. One day when he was 19 months old, I was working in my shop and Nathan was nearby outside the shop with a young guy named Sunbutu who was grinding peanuts. Nathan grabbed a handful of peanuts and stuffed them into his mouth. He then fell from the bench he was sitting on and the peanuts got lodged in his throat. He couldn't swallow them and so he started gagging and choking. I heard the commotion so I rushed outside and saw him struggling to breathe. Following our medical training, I patted his back as hard as I could without hurting him, but the peanuts still wouldn't come out.

We radioed MAF but it was too late in the day for them to fly out to Burji, so we waited anxiously through the night. His breathing was labored, but his color still looked good. The next day we flew to Soddu, where our mission had a hospital. The X-rays didn't show the peanuts, so the doctor put a scope down Nathan's throat, but it actually pushed the peanuts down and blocked his breathing. Nathan didn't make it long after that. The doctor was really a great doctor, but there was nothing he could do to save him. He felt so badly.

The next day we brought Nathan's body back to Burji on a plane. Here's the character of Jeanette. She was so concerned for Sunbutu, she told me that I must tell him it wasn't his fault. Even in her deepest grief, she was concerned for the well-being of others. I'm sure he was terribly sad and scared. She wanted him to know we didn't hold it against him but rather we understood it was somehow in God's plan.

Nathan, a few days before he died

We buried him just below our house. We had a burial service and I spoke for a while. Then the people asked if they could do what they normally did when someone died. So, for three days people came from churches all around just to spend the days with us, to comfort us. At first it seemed overwhelming to have so many people around. We preferred to be alone and busy ourselves with some normal activities. But we decided to let them minister to us, and it became apparent that in doing so, we were actually ministering to them also.

During those days, Jeanette took out a picture of Nathan and showed it around to the people. She began talking about him, saying that someday we would see him again in heaven. They were shocked that she could bring herself to do such a thing. They didn't talk about a person after they had died. She had tears in her eyes, which made all the women tear up as well. I think it gave them some relief to see that the Lord comforts us in our sorrow, but that doesn't mean we don't feel the sorrow. The people served us coffee and roasted grain. It was a way of honoring them – by receiving from them. In the depths of our grief, we were comforting others.

One of the men I grew to really love, Momo, came to me and said, "Now you understand us." He and his wife had lost several children. One family there had lost eight. Grief was such a common experience in the lives of those people. Losing our son was not the way we would have chosen to better understand the people, but it was the way the Lord chose for us. To teach people, you must also understand them. We had come there to teach them and build them in God's Word, and we were simply passing on to them the truth that He was teaching us.

Burial service for Nathan outside our home

7

My Lonely Battle

The Ethiopian highland where we lived was a savanna – rolling hills covered with grasslands and scattered trees. During the dry season the streams would run out of water, but the Guji people who had lived there for centuries knew how to get water for their cattle in that thirsty land. I remember coming upon a water hole, probably thirty feet deep and a hundred feet wide, while visiting the area by mule. I don't know how long it had taken them to dig that hole – perhaps generations – but it was constantly being dug still deeper as its water level receded. To pull the water out of the hole, the people dug stages into the bank slopes where several men stood and passed bucketsful to each other up to the rim, where several more men dumped them into a series of water troughs. What interested me was seeing how many men it took to get the water up to the top of the hole. It would have been impossible for just one man to perform that by himself.

This is how I sometimes felt during the early years of our time in Ethiopia. I was working mostly alone in ministry outside the home while Jeanette worked at home with the kids. I was constantly giving but seldom receiving any spiritual refreshment, outside of what I got during my personal devotions. I longed for a friend with a kindred heart for God – someone who could help me quench my thirst for Him. For a long time I didn't even know what my heart was crying out for. I had grown up to be very independent and I hadn't made many close friends, so I was used to being alone. But I began to realize that I desired something more when I started feeling so dissatisfied with the level of fellowship I was experiencing with the other missionaries I knew. It wasn't that they weren't good people. They were very good people and I knew they all loved the Lord. But when we got together, we mainly discussed our work. We didn't talk about the deep things of God that I was thirsting for. Maybe they were longing for the same thing that I wanted, but we never got around to talking about it. We were always too busy planning or taking care of our physical provisions to enter into a deep spiritual conversation. But it left me feeling dissatisfied and my spiritual thirst just kept increasing. I was crying out to the Lord to satisfy my thirst, but I didn't know how to express my need to anyone else.

Looking back, I can see how the Lord was actually answering my prayer while He was also preparing me to become an answer to someone else's prayer. The answer didn't come until we'd been in Ethiopia for six or seven years, but it did come.

I was not the only one who was feeling isolated at our station. An older single missionary lady often came to our home in the evening and she would just talk and talk for hours. She didn't want to listen. She just wanted to talk. If you started to say something, she'd interrupt and remark how it reminded her of something else, and then she'd take the conversation in a whole new direction. I have never been a very good listener myself, so that was way too much for me. Jeanette was a lot more patient in listening to her, but she also had the kids to look after, so she wasn't always in the room. I usually had a few copies of *Popular Mechanics* lying around, so I'd pick one up and start reading it while she was still talking. Now and then I'd look up from the magazine and nod like I was agreeing with something she'd said, but then I'd go back to reading. It may have been impolite to do that, but it was my only way of coping with the burden I was feeling.

That lady was a wonderful missionary. She'd been in the country for many years before we came and she had a terrific rapport with the people. She was serving the Lord under great personal sacrifice. But it shows you what loneliness can do to a person out in a remote station. She was thirsting for company, but I don't know if she ever got what she was wanting. At least, she didn't get it very well from me.

I suppose I was getting a dose of my own medicine from her. I didn't listen well, but I was looking to find deep fellowship with others where it wasn't to be found. It seemed like my pleas were falling on deaf ears. So I kept trying to go deeper with the Lord on my own, and He used my pursuit to make me even thirstier for Him.

Jeanette was struggling in her own way. To begin with, losing Nathan was a loss we would never get over. It was a continuing grief, with fresh reminders. While I busied myself with many responsibilities at the Bible school and in the field, Jeanette was committed to the home and to our children. When I returned from trips, I was excited to tell her everything the Lord had done. She wanted to share with me something she had been facing. Gradually, she began to feel like she wasn't contributing anything of real significance to the mission. The nurse on the compound had her job and the teacher had hers, but Jeanette started to feel like her work wasn't as important. I wasn't listening to her. I just discounted it, thinking she should be listening to me telling her all I was doing.

But I wasn't fully appreciating what she was doing either. Jeanette was always, first and foremost, a mother. We had young children with us from the very start of our ministry there. Some missionary children suffered with parents overly involved in ministry. I did not want that. Jeanette and I both felt it was her first priority to be home with the kids, not neglecting them. Her ministry to people flowed out of the home. Jeanette was hospitable to the people who came to our home. She never turned anyone away even when she was busy. She would make up some sweet tea and pop some American popcorn on the wood stove. She also taught some of the young girls how to sew by hand and other practical things. Jeanette taught the Bible in Sunday school as well as a women's Bible class. She also wrote out Bible questions in Amharic for my lessons. Her handwriting is much better than mine. Jeanette was very caring and compassionate. She was a helper in every way, and she could really make people feel at home.

Melodie joining Jeanette's sewing class

Gradually I came to realize that, as the head of our home, I was the priest of our household and I needed to heed that God-given responsibility. It struck me that when I went away I was leaving my wife and children spiritually unguarded from the enemy's attacks. So I began to seriously pray for them before I left home and while I was away. I consciously turned them over to the Lord for His protection, trusting Him to be Jeanette's husband and our children's father while I was gone. From that time on, it dramatically changed how well things went in our home when I was gone.

One of those times when I was on a trip Jeanette had an unusual challenge at home and she needed the Lord's direct protection. During the night, two-year-old Melodie needed to go to the bathroom. While she was sitting on her little potty chair, Jeanette noticed a snake lying on the floor between Melodie and her. She didn't say a word to Melodie, afraid that might startle her and cause her to jump at the snake. Instead she reached out and grabbed Melodie's hand, pulling her through the doorway, and slammed the door shut. She heard the snake violently striking against it.

The next day a worker came and Jeanette told him about the snake. He opened the door and found it dead. It had been crushed by the door when Jeanette had slammed it shut. He said it was a very poisonous variety. She thanked God for His protection.

The more seriously I took my role as priest of my household, the more aware I became when I needed to pray for them while I was away. I realized that Jeanette and the children were also targets in the spiritual battle we were facing. I would often return and tell Jeanette I had felt strongly impressed to pray for her at a certain time and she would tell me how hard things had been at home and that suddenly the trouble had died down. I told her I was praying just at that hour.

I had never had any direct experience in dealing with the demon possessed, but that changed soon after we arrived in Burji. Some of the tribes held ritual ceremonies, presenting four-year-old girls to receive their demon guides. The demons didn't guide them; they controlled them.

The worst case of a demon-possessed woman that I encountered was also the first case I encountered. The woman's name was Mamiti. She was probably in her 30's, but looked much older. Mamiti came to us wearing a worn-out, filthy dress. She was skinny and scrawny, but she was tremendously strong. She had been bound in chains and yet broke them with ease. It took seven strong men to hold her down – just barely. One time the villagers had chained her to a chair in a hut to keep her from bothering others, but she broke the chains and dug by hand under the walls and freed herself.

Mamiti just wandered from place to place after she had worn out her welcome. That never took long. We heard she'd been poisoned by some Muslims who were trying to kill her at the place she'd been before she wandered into Burji. She was really crazy and unpredictable, but she came to us for refuge from all the beatings and ill treatment she had received from others.

When Mamiti first came to Burji, she used to crawl beneath our house and sleep there at night. We took pity on her and tried to be kind to her. We fed her and we let her sleep beneath our house. But it soon became apparent that she was both gross and dangerous. Reenie started having terrible nightmares. She was so frightened, she couldn't even cry out. When she finally told me about this, I realized we had a horrible situation on our hands.

I hesitate to even mention this, but one of the disgusting things Mamiti did was she sucked the mucous from the nose of Debbie, our

Mamiti, a demon possessed woman who slept under our house

fourth daughter, when she had a cold. She just sucked it up and spit it out. It was so vile. Then she started threatening to throw our kids into the toilet hole in the outhouse or run away with them. We kept our kids away from her but it added a lot of stress in our home to have her around. One day she went into my shop and took two liters of motor oil and drank them both. It was running right through her. I don't know why it didn't kill her, but it was foul. A couple times she stripped naked and stood on our Land Rover with arms raised to the moon. We never knew what she was going to do next.

The Bible school students were also kind to her. We held several intense prayer sessions over her, but I think it just made her feel more agitated. I really didn't know how to deal with her, except I realized through reading Scripture that I didn't need to be afraid of the demons because the power of Christ in me is greater than the power of Satan in her.

Mamiti stayed around, harassed and crazy, for about a month before she wandered off again. To my knowledge, she never surrendered to Christ. I later heard that she had somehow found her way to a place about 100 miles from us where someone had killed her.

That was one of the more obvious ways that Satan showed himself. Even though I didn't yet really know how to cast out Satan from a person, it was in some ways easier to deal with the obvious manifestations of evil than it was to deal with the more subtle attacks. When we found it necessary to raise the fees at the Bible school by just a little, some of the students resisted very strongly. There were just a few who were really critical, but the negativity began to permeate the whole atmosphere. As I've mentioned, students there were generally very respectful of instructors, but some began to get argumentative. I started to wonder if I should just close the Bible school for a year. Instead I kept it open, hoping things would change, but I kept getting more resistance. This went on for two or three years, making it harder for me to teach. I was beginning to think my time at Burji was coming to a close. I figured I had probably done all I could do.

In need of encouragement, my desire for a like-minded friend intensified, but I also realized I had a real spiritual ally in my own wife. Jeanette was always one to pray for me. The spiritual battle was too intense for me to neglect the help He had already given to me in her. Later after we left Burji, I met a man whose spiritual thirst was as deep as my own. He was the kind of friend I had been seeking.

8
Getting a Leg Up on Suffering

When you're getting bombarded by difficulties, it's normal to wonder whether you really are where God wants you to be. When all your norms are nowhere to be found – your language, your routine, your friends and your family – even minor inconveniences can add up to major culture shock. One couple decided to leave the country because the man's wife couldn't accept the thought of raising kids in a place where there was so much sickness and filth. She struggled with fear regarding their children. I can't judge her because she was probably right. What mother wouldn't be concerned about exposing her children to disease? Her husband wasn't as concerned about that. He felt called to Ethiopia. But she didn't feel called to live there, so that ended their time there. I was blessed to know that Jeanette knew she was called along with me to serve the Lord in Ethiopia. At times, it was only this awareness that kept us there.

After losing Nathan, the possibility of losing another child seemed more real and more terrible to us. We were well aware that if it could happen once, it could happen again. And because we had gone through the pain of it, we were acutely aware of how hard it would be the next time. If Satan wanted to defeat us on the mission field, our children were our tender spots. But it was Jeanette's tender heart for our children that also made her so tough in her prayers. She was always on prayer alert for them. There were several occasions when her prayers clearly prevailed over Satan's attacks.

Melodie and Reenie were little ones when we were first at Burji. This meant they were always running around and getting into things. Once when Jeanette and I were away at an early-morning prayer meeting at another missionary's home, we left them with a worker to look after them. When we returned, for some reason Jeanette looked into our bedroom closet and happened to look into a box of shoes on the floor. She didn't even know why she did that, but we praised the Lord she did. When she looked into it, she discovered the "baby-proof" lid on a bottle of baby aspirin had been opened and most of the tablets were gone. She immediately questioned the girls. Melodie denied all wrongdoing. But Reenie admitted to swallowing lots of them.

Jeanette went to the mission nurse and told her what had happened. They were soon on the two-way radio with a mission doctor who gave instructions to make a concoction of eggs and other ingredients that was supposed to make her vomit. But Reenie's stomach was too tough. She wouldn't vomit. So the nurse had to run a tube down Reenie's throat and into her stomach. That took lots of doing – me holding her tightly while the nurse was working the tube down her throat and Jeanette was "praying like 60." Reenie was crying and squirming the whole time. I did all I could to hold on to her without hurting her. Finally all that pink fluid came gushing out. We thanked God.

But the drug was still in Reenie's system, so the doctor told us to keep her awake and alert for many hours. We couldn't let her nap, so Jeanette stayed with her all day, reading stories over and over to her while quietly praying for her the whole time. She soon recovered from her trauma. Quite a while later, Melodie confessed that she too had previously "enjoyed" a mouthful of baby aspirin. But thankfully, God had intervened and she had no ill effects from it.

As most parents might say, it's a miracle that kids survive a normal childhood. But it was an even bigger miracle that our kids survived on the mission field. On another occasion, when Melodie was still a preschooler, she became listless, lying on the couch with no energy to get up and play. This went on for quite a while. So when we were in Addis Ababa, we took her to a government hospital for a checkup. Nothing unusual showed up in her blood work. Back in Burji, she was still the same – just languishing around. Of course, Jeanette was on prayer alert, so when we made another trip to Addis, the Lord prompted her to take along a list of meds Melodie had taken for a variety of problems she'd had. Sure enough, the doctor took one look at that list and had it figured out – she'd been ingesting too many meds for her little body. He told us to keep her off all meds unless she was deathly ill. He instructed us to give her no sweets, but instead only wholesome food. That's all it took for her to get back to full energy. But that wasn't really all it took – it took a lot of prayer and God's amazing grace and love, watching over us and our little girl.

Our first furlough was good for Jeanette and me. It had been over four years since we had seen our families. Jeanette's folks met us for a wonderful week in Sweden with relatives, on our return trip to the States. Even though furlough times were very busy, filled with speaking to various church groups, it was good to connect with people again and to connect in our own language. We knew we needed people praying for us. There was no sense in us returning to Ethiopia, if people were not praying. It was during this furlough that Shari, our third daughter, was born.

After we returned to Ethiopia, it was obvious that Melodie and Reenie were glad to be back. Africa was their true home. So within the first hour after our arrival in Burji, they rushed outside and climbed the guava tree in our back yard. While they were scrambling up the tree in their Sunday shoes, we cautioned them to be careful. The words were still falling from our lips when Reenie lost her grip and came tumbling down and landed squarely on her nose. The missionary nurse, welcoming us back from furlough, happened to be right there with us.

We called the pilot to see if he could return and take us to the mission hospital in Sheshamane, but it was too late in the day for a flight to come in. We needed to keep a close eye on Reenie, so she stayed that night in our room. I'm sure we didn't get a wink all night, praying most of the time.

The next morning the plane came in and Jeanette went off with Reenie and baby Shari to the mission station. When the doctor saw Reenie, he said too much time had passed to stitch her nose. It would have to heal by itself. Her nose was broken. It would also be necessary to wait for the swelling and bruising to subside, so he could make sure things were healing correctly. They stayed there for several days. Reenie's face was so damaged by her injury that Jeanette kept her from seeing herself in a mirror, for fear that she would be frightened. But she caught a glimpse of her face in a shiny toaster, and it did scare her. She wondered if she would ever look like herself again. But she did recover and regain her sweet face. And once again, we rejoiced in God's continued care and grace in time of need.

These kinds of stories alone could fill a book, but I will add just one more. One Sunday morning, I decided to let Jeanette go to church for a needed break from her constant care of the kids. I busied myself with some small tasks while little Shari was in my arms, not feeling well. When Jeanette returned, she picked her up. By then Shari was completely out of it. She didn't respond at all to Jeanette's voice. Her eyes were rolled back in her head. It scared Jeanette and she kept trying to wake her saying, "Mommy's home! It's okay, Shari. You'll feel better soon." But she knew that something was desperately wrong with her.

That's when Jeanette began to pray in the way that mothers who have already lost a child pray. She reminded God that we already had a grave in our front yard and we didn't want another one.

It's hard to say how long Shari was totally out of it, but it seemed like forever. Finally she started coming to a little. We contacted our SIM mission headquarters in Addis and they wanted us to bring her in on a flight the next day. So Jeanette took her, while I stayed home with Melodie and Reenie.

The doctor took so many blood samples that Shari's arms looked like pincushions. She became deathly afraid of needles, and it took her years to get over it. After a number of blood tests, they concluded that Shari might have a serious blood disorder. From the medical training we had received at Biola, Jeanette immediately wondered if it might be leukemia, which would require a bone marrow puncture to verify. That is a painful procedure we didn't want Shari to endure.

The day before the procedure was scheduled to occur, Jeanette called the hospital to find out when they needed to be there. The person on the phone told her, "Just a minute. The blood results from yesterday showed a slight improvement. Come instead for another blood test."

The following blood tests showed continued improvement. So Shari never needed to get that bone marrow test. We joyfully thanked the Lord for this. And Shari was soon back to normal, running all around, yet calm and happy as always. Obviously God was listening when Jeanette reminded Him that we already had one grave in our front yard, and we didn't want another.

Nevertheless, we realized that when we signed up to follow the Lord to Ethiopia, we were signing up for some hardships. It was just the way it was, both for ourselves and for the people we were called to reach with the gospel. It came with the territory. Many times when I began to feel that missionary life was too tough, I thought of soldiers out in the sand, their head against a tire as they tried to sleep. If the soldier lives that way, should not the soldier of the cross be able to go through these different things, whether it is sickness, fleas, rats, or even death and sorrow? The Apostle Paul, who had suffered for the sake of the gospel, wrote to Timothy, "Endure hardship as a good soldier of Jesus Christ."[12] God often gave me that thought and then I was fine. I had grown up enduring hardship. It was just a way of life for me, and God used it all to prepare me for the mission field as well as to remind me to persevere through the many hardships that came.

When we got to Ethiopia, I realized I had never had it very hard at all compared to most people in the world. I saw how the students in our Bible school would sacrifice, even running barefoot for hours up and down the mountains to get to school. They didn't have money. They just lived on bare necessities. And then they would go back to their very hard lives in the villages and work to scrape a living from their farms.

But as I discovered, suffering for the gospel's sake can come in various forms. As I traveled the countryside, building actual church buildings for the people, the way to the work was sometimes hazardous. I was riding my motorcycle through the bush somewhere beyond Burji when my leg got nicked by something sharp, probably a thorn. By the time I got to the site, my leg was throbbing and was infected. A huge ulcer formed on my leg and I got very feverish. We were about a five-hour run from Burji where I could get an antibiotic. One of the fastest runners went after it. Meanwhile, I had to wait in pain. But figuring I'd be in pain whether waiting or working, I decided to work while I waited. I climbed up on the roof to work alongside a coworker and just kept my leg elevated. I knew how to work while suffering, identifying with the nationals.

As missionaries, we struggled with what we considered hardships, but compared to the nationals, we were really a bunch of softies. We gave of ourselves, but they gave even more for the gospel. And the way they gave was phenomenal. They had no money, but at conferences they gave chickens and other animals or produce from their farms, even the sweater or shirt on their backs – things that could be exchanged for cash. And they gave cheerfully. I say this not to minimize the sacrifice of missionaries, but to view it from a broader perspective. They had seen their own children dying, and as my friend Momo had told me, it was when our son Nathan died that he knew we could truly understand them. We brought to them an understanding of the gospel, and they gave to us a greater understanding of what it means to suffer for it.

Having a Bible study with believers we worked with in Burji

9
Brothers of the Heart

Ethiopia has been struck by many famines throughout its history. Most of them have occurred in the northern part of the country, where the weather is hot and dry. But I recall one year, in the middle of the growing season, when a plague of grasshoppers devoured the crops near Burji. The people in our area were mostly farmers, each family holding a plot of land for growing wheat, teff seeds, corn and coffee. One day I was looking down at the distant green hillsides and the grasshoppers came in like a dark cloud. The next day I looked in the same direction and the hills were completely brown. In a single day, the crops were gone.

We grieved and prayed with the people. It was a devastating loss. They had worked hard for their harvests and it was very important for their livelihood. But there was nothing we could do to help them. All they could do was wait for the next planting season and start over. They would go back to cultivating the soil by hand with long iron bars. It was back-breaking work and they would go at it for weeks at a time. And there could always be another devastation again the next year. It was such a hard life, but it was the only life they knew. I don't know how they survived under those conditions.

Then there were the Guji Gala nomadic peoples who lived in the Segen Valley. They were cattle herders. Their cattle were prone to sleeping sickness. It was fatal if not treated with the proper antidotes. Fortunately, I was able to acquire a supply of vials of medication and syringes from Addis to inject the animals, which saved many cattle and helped many, many people.

This was the nature of our work there. We helped as many people as we could, and we grieved over the many that we couldn't help. It was sometimes overwhelming, but I never regretted being there. No matter how hard it got, I was aware of the Lord's presence.

But there were many days at the Bible school when I would walk home discouraged and console my heart by singing, *"There is a place of quiet rest, near to the heart of God."* I really needed that

A monolithic anthill while traveling by mule among the Guji people

quiet rest in my heart because it was not to be found in my situation. Some of the students were grumbling about my leadership. Off in the distance, there were rumblings of a communist takeover. While most of that disturbance was still far away from us, we had to have an exit plan should things get too volatile. When we started the Bible school, there were only five or six students, but God had blessed the school and there were about fifty students after three years. As a result, our influence was noticeably growing. But it is not always helpful to be noticed. Church leaders were often put in prison.

One of our students, a young man named Tirufat, became a leader among the youth in our area. He was very intelligent and a very sharp student, a real bright spot in my class. I used to joke around with him and I really enjoyed his spirit. The communists were trying to recruit all the young people for their collective farms, especially Christians, because they were trustworthy and would not undermine their efforts. Tirufat had a much bigger following than the communists, so he was considered a threat to them. He was harassed and eventually arrested.

But that didn't stop him from witnessing to other political prisoners. In fact, the number of Christians increased in the prisons. When wives and mothers brought the prisoners food, they also smuggled Bibles to them. Then Bible studies began to form behind the prison walls. The communists didn't want too many Christians in one prison, so they sent them to other prisons. In dispersing the believers, the communists were actually aiding the spread of the gospel.

Just like the farmers who had lost their crops and the herdsmen who lost their cattle, Tirufat kept living for Jesus even in the hardest of times. I admired him for this.

Despite the threatening conditions around us, the work was growing. Together with other SIM missionaries, we arranged conferences way out in the bush, teaching church leaders from Romans and other books of the Bible. Sometimes 300 leaders from over 70 churches gathered at a single conference. I enjoyed those gatherings more than the Bible school. I enjoyed going out to the people, but it also drained me to be around people all day long.

I liked working with my hands, finishing a task without any interruptions, but that seldom happened. Guys were always bringing me their old Italian rifles that needed to be repaired. Growing up on the farm, we did a lot of hunting, so I was always fixing a rifle or a gun. I enjoyed doing it on my own without anybody around me. Fixing things gave my mind a break from all the people problems. But usually they'd bring a rifle to me unannounced and then stay around to watch and ask questions while I worked. It was stressful for me because when people came to visit me, they expected me to give them my undivided attention. I wanted to be sociable but I also didn't work well when someone was talking to me. I felt like I needed time away from people, so I could be refreshed enough to meet with a class of students the next day.

The communists inadvertently helped me out of my dilemma. Even though the rifles were being used only for hunting, I didn't want to be accused by the communists of being an arms supplier, so I had to stop fixing them. I fixed all kinds of other things for people, but I stopped fixing guns.

I've already mentioned how legalistic the Burji and Quara believers were. It troubled me to know that their evangelists were spreading their legalism among the Guji people. They had completely different tribal backgrounds, with totally different languages and customs. And yet, the Burji and the Quara insisted that their traditions must be followed. They looked and dressed differently than the Guji. But in bringing the gospel to them, they also tried to change their culture. For instance, the Guji women put rancid butter in their hair. You could smell it a mile away, but they liked it that way. The evangelists wanted to change the way they dressed. They also tried to stop them from piercing their cows and drinking the blood and eating raw meat. These were matters of health, not matters of gospel truth. I could see the real need for the gospel of grace to be preached among the Guji, but I couldn't do much about it because I was so busy working with the legalistic churches and in the Bible school.

We tried to address the problem of legalism and other serious matters, but we were met with a lot of resistance. One man started spreading the idea that we didn't care about the churches that were in the highlands because we seldom visited them. They were located in very remote areas and it was very difficult to get to them. There were just too many churches and too few missionaries. Around that time, 45 churches broke off from SIM and joined with the Norwegian Lutherans. Some eventually returned to us, but most just disappeared.

So, inside the church we had legalism to contend with and outside the church we had the danger of communism. Like grasshoppers devouring the crops, both threatened to ruin the work we were trying to accomplish in the Burji area.

The Gadeo people had been conquered years earlier by the Amhara people. Haile Selassie was the Amhara leader. He had gone to the British and asked them to push out the Italians from Ethiopia. He was very grateful for their help and so he allowed them to bring in some missionaries. They helped the country by establishing schools and hospitals. Of course, the national language became Amharic, which further embittered the Gadeo. So the Gadeo joined with the communists to push back the Amharas. The missionaries were caught in the middle of it all.

Jeanette and I had been praying and talking about possibly moving on from Burji. After seven years or so, it seemed I had done all I could do in the area. There was a station at Dilla, about a day's drive closer to Addis, where I could work closely with the churches. It would also bring us much closer to Bingham Academy, where the girls were staying in school.

It was hard for me to think about leaving, even with all the

Dropping Melodie and Reenie off at Bingham Academy

difficulties. But it was easier to think of being closer to our girls. This was especially so for Jeanette. It would have been dreadful to be so far away from them in the case of a national emergency, such as a civil war. And it was becoming more and more clear that a communist takeover and civil war were brewing.

It was during this time that the words of that song, *"There is a place of quiet rest, near to the heart of God,"* kept me going. It kept me coming back to enjoying my rest in the Lord. But I still didn't know how to deal with the conflict and resistance I was experiencing in the school. I wished for a friend, someone who could listen and counsel me. And while the Lord was making me aware of my need, He was also providing the solution.

A man named Albert Brandt, a SIM missionary, had come to Ethiopia in 1947. As the story goes, there was a medicine man named Wirasa in Ethiopia who had a vision of white people riding on donkeys, stopping under a big bay tree and setting up tents. From there they built buildings with shiny roofs. Tin roofs were unknown at that time. In the vision, the medicine man was told that the white people would tell him about Muhgano, the God of Creation. Not long afterward, Wirasa came to Dilla. He became Mrs. Brandt's first literacy student. He heard the gospel and recognized that his vision had been fulfilled. Through Wirasa's conversion and influence, the church grew and spread throughout the area. Albert Brandt started the work in Dilla.

I had met the Brandt's son, Howie, on a few occasions at SIM conferences. We had also crossed paths a couple times in the States. Howie was also a Prairie graduate. We fell into conversation at a conference and it soon became apparent to both of us that we were brothers of the same spirit and heart. Howie was a dynamic teacher, and I invited him to come to one of our rural conferences in the mountains. I hauled him up there on the back of my motorcycle. We stayed in a tent and we talked; we sang and prayed together. It was amazing how well we clicked. It also affected my experience during the conference. I felt strongly encouraged. Knowing I was sharing the experience with a good friend, I enjoyed the people all the more.

One thing I especially recall is the antiphonal singing of the people. One guy would lead the people in song while everybody would repeat the same phrase over and over. He'd be telling them a story in the song and they would respond. It was beautiful to see them expressing worship like that in their own language and culture. The people were in tears. I couldn't understand the story, but I could understand their hearts were worshiping the Lord.

Howie and I set up our tent inside the church building. Before the start of every session, we prayed together. I could sense his love and zeal for the Lord and for the people he was ministering to. He was so sincere in committing the whole evening to the Lord, fully surrendering himself and pouring out his heart to Him. God really moved among the people. There was real power in Howie's messages. I remember thinking, "This man really knows how to pray!" Howie also heard me praying and he later told me he had thought the same about me.

Howie was serving further north and we were in the south, so we didn't see each other often, maybe once or twice a year. But I knew I had found the friend I had been longing for. We both wanted to go deeper with the Lord and we held a weeklong retreat for other missionaries to go deeper with us. As glad as we were when devastating droughts diminished in Ethiopia, our hearts still thirsted as much for the living God. Finally, the long dry spell I had endured, praying for a like-minded brother, seemed to have come to an end.

10
Bumbling is Humbling

As Jeanette and I prayed about the possibility of leaving Burji, I wrestled with the reality that the churches in the area were still quite weak and shallow. I wanted to see my students growing stronger and deeper in the Word, both in understanding and in

Enjoying time with Bible school students, eating roasted wheat

practice. I was thankful for the leaders we were training at the Bible school, but even after several years of teaching, I still felt limited in my ability to express myself, and I felt that my limitations were also limiting my students.

The best stage for impacting students is not the classroom. It is in their own surroundings. So I was always excited whenever a student invited me to visit the church in his area, and I was eager to have a greater impact on their lives.

A pastor named Tadessa invited me to his village for a baptism ceremony. He was a good man and a good student. He was just the kind of man I wanted to influence for the Lord. I felt honored to be invited to this occasion and he was happy when I accepted his invitation. As his honored guest, I was expected to stay in Tadessa's home and receive the royal treatment. He had really spruced up his place. He had covered the cracks in the walls with fresh cow manure to help keep the bed bugs and the fleas from being so plentiful. After the baptism ceremony, we returned to his home at about 11 that evening for a meal. Smoke from a fire in the middle of the room permeated the air and Tadessa

Baptism in the Burji area

happily announced to me, "We want to offer you a calf." He wanted to kill his only calf for our meal.

I knew he was very poor, and I knew what a great sacrifice that would be for him and his family, so I politely declined his offer. I didn't realize I was making a terrible cultural mistake. Tadessa intended his sacrifice to be a celebration, a gesture of generosity that was suitable to his guest of honor. He kept insisting that I accept his offer and I kept politely refusing. To make matters worse, I told him, "No, I don't want to accept anything from you."

Tadessa was deeply offended. By my refusal of his offer, he felt that I was saying he had nothing of value to offer me, which meant that I was putting myself above him. That was the furthest thing from my mind, but to him I was sounding prideful. He pleaded with me to accept the calf, but I kept saying no. Finally, he gave up and went to bed.

Tadessa had laid an animal skin on the floor for me to sleep on. I spread my sleeping bag on it and crawled inside. Before long I realized the skin was infested with fleas. They were invading my sleeping bag and biting me all over my body. I squirmed and twitched and pulled myself deep inside the bag, but I couldn't stay in there for long because it got so hot and stuffy I could barely breathe. Meanwhile, Tadessa and his family were sleeping soundly. I suppose they were immune to the fleabites.

While I was tossing about in my sleeping bag, big rats were running around the house and crawling among the thatches in the roof. I could hear them clawing and scampering. I hate rats, so I buried myself back inside my sleeping bag. But again, it got hot and stuffy in there, so I had to come out for a breath of air. I tossed and turned for hours. Finally I fell asleep. But then I was aroused again. My arm was dangling out of the bag and I felt something heavy on my hand. I felt it moving. Suddenly I realized what it was. A rat! I freaked and tossed it across the room. It landed right on top of Marge Langford, an older missionary who had come for the baptism. She let out a yelp. This was not the kind of impression I was hoping to make on Tadessa in his own surroundings.

I most enjoyed getting out into the surrounding villages where I felt I could be most effective in the churches, but there were rats everywhere. When I went to conferences, typically we would eat at midnight or 1:00 am. After we had bedded down, I could hear the rats cleaning up the crumbs and leftovers from our meal. On one occasion, there were more than a hundred conference participants sleeping on the floor of a large church. Again, I was tucked inside my sleeping bag and it was hot and stale in the room. I struggled to fall asleep. Then I awoke with something heavy on my head. I opened my eyes and saw a huge rat sitting right on my face. I flung it as far as I could. I was just thankful I didn't have leprosy, as many Ethiopians did. If I had been a leper, the rat might have eaten my nose without me knowing it until the next morning.

Gradually I learned from my cultural mistakes, and I kept myself from getting eaten alive by rats and fleas. But it was also eating at me deep inside to be leaving the people before I had finished my job there. I could see that my best work was not in the classroom. I was at my best when I was out among the people in their own surroundings, in spite of the pests and my cultural blunders. I was thankful that I had learned to build things on the stump ranch where I had grown up. That gave me a good way to help the people without making too many miscues. But as much as I wanted to give to the people, I also learned that I needed to be willing to receive from them.

When I visited the Guji people, I was sometimes invited inside their grass huts, which were flimsy temporary shelters where they stayed before herding their cattle to greener pastures. It was dark inside those huts, except for a fire burning in the middle of the floor. The air was filled with both smoke and friendliness. The host handed me a dug out wooden cup teeming with hot cow's milk covered with roasted coffee beans. The shells were still on the beans which floated on the top of the drink. I had a hard time drinking the stuff because it required both chewing and swallowing at once. It tasted good, but I couldn't keep the shells from getting stuck between my teeth. With a mouthful of grit, I'm sure my smile looked pretty crusty, but I could see the pleasure they had in serving me that delicacy. And I could see that I needed to let them serve me with their gifts so that I could serve them with mine.

Drinking hot cow's milk with the Guji people

This is why I felt my influence for the Lord was more real and lasting in the field than it was in the classroom. Out there, I was not the expert. I was still a learner. I needed to apply what the Scriptures say, which only reminded me of how much I needed God's grace every moment. Sometimes I would be appalled at my mistakes, and yet I found it to be another stepping stone toward a deeper humility and a more genuine relationship with the Lord. Nothing humbles a believer more than his or her own sins and failures. It's one thing to teach the Scriptures, and another thing to live by them. My dad used to tell me this. I'd be all excited about memorizing a passage, and then he'd ask me how I was going to apply what I had memorized. That's why going to the conferences and the churches out in the bush was so exciting to me. After sitting under all the great teaching I had heard at Prairie concerning God's grace and many other great truths, sound theory and good theology were not enough to see me through the challenges and failures I faced. Out there, I needed to be a doer of the Word, not just a teacher.

One of the humbling lessons I needed to learn was how to receive from others. The Lord took me through that long dry spell so that I could realize my need for a friend like Howie – a friend I respected and trusted enough to receive from. But I also needed to learn to receive from those who seemed to have little to offer me, at least in my eyes. I was too independent and individualistic to take what others had to offer me. I thought it was up to me to do all the giving. But I was learning that, as a servant leader, I needed to let others serve me also.

The people often saw me making cultural messes and they were forgiving. It was also necessary to let them make messes of their own. Jeanette really helped me with this. The Ethiopians are very hospitable people and they also enjoyed visiting with us in our home. I think some missionaries felt uneasy when small national children came into their homes and sat on their furniture because they sometimes had accidents wherever they happened to be sitting. We were not big social bugs ourselves, but we did feel it was important to keep our door open to everyone, including the students and children. We sometimes held parties for them, which meant a lot of spills and splatter. But that is when Jeanette really shined. She was exceptionally patient and kind. Those kinds of mishaps didn't bother her. After all, she was a mother of five children, as Debbie and Joycie had now joined the clan. So we got grace and we gave grace. That's what grace is for – to give and to receive.

I had always been a doer, and as long as I was busy and felt effective in ministry, I felt good about myself. But busyness is not the best way to measure success in ministry. When I came home from a conference or from visiting a village church, I was full of stories that I wanted to tell Jeanette. But she had stories of her own – stories of her struggles with the daily challenges of living in Ethiopia while raising small children, wondering what contribution

All five daughters from left to right:
Melodie, Joycie, Reenie, Shari and Debbie

she was making as a missionary. But then through reading *The Missionary Wife and Her Work,* a book her sister had sent her, and through Howie, who listened well, she came to realize it was God who gave her the role she had as a wife and mother; she didn't need to compare or explain herself to anyone. Wherever God placed her and whatever He gave her to do, He would supply her grace to do just that and only that. I had been trying to tell her the same thing in my own way, but I was mixing up the message because I was still trying to get her to listen to me, rather than listening to her. Coming from Howie, the message seemed to get through to her because he had no expectations of her. The lessons of grace are best taught and caught when we have no expectations of our own.

I used to get into discussions and debates with other missionaries about the content of our Bible school teaching. To me, the lessons seemed too academic. The goal had to go beyond teaching students how to take a test. Maybe it was just that I am not gifted in that way. I am very practical and I want to know how everything works in real life, whether it's a car engine or a passage of Scripture. Sometimes I may be too practical and not very thoughtful or considerate of others. But I do know we can study to get all the right answers and still not know the right answer.

An older man who attended the Bible school before I arrived used to answer "Jesus" on every test question. When asked about his repeated answers, he simply replied, "Jesus is the answer to everything." We used to laugh about that.

He didn't pass the exams, but he was right about Jesus.

11

"You Go For Me"

I had already put in a request to leave Burji when we left for our second furlough in 1975. An opening in Dilla had come up which appealed to me in many ways, but the final decision for our placement was in the hands of the SIM governing council.

The nearer distance from Dilla to Addis Ababa, where Bingham Academy was located, was a strong factor for us because it brought us a day's drive closer to the girls at school. Dilla was our usual stopping point between Burji and Addis. The road from there to Addis was much better than the stretch from Burji to Dilla. It was also our connecting point to Ethiopia when we first started raising funds to become missionaries. A longtime SIM missionary named Dean Jongeward had worked for many years among the Gadeo people in the region around Dilla. He was also from the state of Washington, and he had loaned me many of his slides and stories to tell to potential supporters. That was very helpful to me.

Dean was back home in Yakima when we were on furlough, so I went to see him. He was dying from brain cancer. He was very weak and could hardly speak, but he raised his head from his bed and said to me, "John, I can't go back to Dilla. You go for me."

I took his charge as a great honor. Dean was a great missionary. He was dynamic and beloved by the people. He was a great communicator and a true disciple-maker. If there was any man's work that I wanted to build upon, it would be Dean's. I knew the Lord had used Dean to build a solid foundation for the churches among the Gadeo. They were well-taught and well-grounded in the Word. To me, it was like hearing God's voice when Dean asked me to go to Dilla. I was thrilled at the possibility of being placed there.

So I presented my case to the board for placing us at Dilla. I wasn't surprised when they told us that's where we were going. The churches in that region were more mature and more plentiful than in the Burji area. I would be responsible for overseeing 120 churches, a big increase from the 70 churches in the Burji district. But the area was more densely populated than it was at Burji, so I wouldn't have to travel as far between churches. The climate was also favorable – Dilla was a thousand feet lower than Burji, so it was warmer. But more importantly, the spiritual climate was better among the Gadeo.

The work there had deeper roots, starting in about 1947 with Howie Brandt's father, Albert, who had preached the gospel there with such force that the people turned from idols and were freed from demonic strongholds. On the top of a nearby mountain there had been some great, tall trees, which the people had worshiped for generations. It was a site where the witch doctors practiced black magic and cast spells upon the people. But as a result of Christ coming into their lives, the people no longer feared the witch doctors and they had boldly cut down those trees during a grand celebration.

The district was divided into two halves, each containing about 120 churches. I was asked to supervise the northern portion. I was to be an advisor to the church leaders, helping to facilitate training courses, arranging the teaching conferences among the churches, sitting on the council of churches and supervising the Bible School, which was much smaller than the school in Burji. This was surprising to me at first. But I was actually relieved. There were some Ethiopians who were teaching there, and they did a good job. They didn't need my help. This freed me up to do what I felt burdened to do. Like Dean Jongeward, I was a disciple-maker, not a teacher or an evangelist. My calling was to build into the lives of leaders, and this new assignment in Dilla would allow me to do primarily that.

The Dilla area was perfect for coffee growing. The rainfall was heavier and there were lots of tall trees to shade the smaller coffee trees. Most people farmed on a few acres and did reasonably well. They were better off than the poorer folks living in and beyond Burji. The churches were also doing well by comparison. They weren't nearly as legalistic as the Burji churches. The average church had about 100 people and some were as large as 800, which was actually a cluster of smaller churches in a close area. This meant our teaching conferences were considerably larger than what I was used to seeing in Burji. They ranged in attendance from 300 to 1,000. The people gathered at those conferences under massive thatched or banana leaf structures for shade and shelter.

The large church in the area, compared to the small Bible school, strengthened my conviction that the church could only

Baptism after a conference

grow deeper and broader by focusing on discipleship, especially among the leadership. This is how I felt called to serve, and I was thankful to be building on the strong foundation that Dean Jongeward had laid before me.

The solid teaching of the Word of God was the main reason for the church's strength. The believers there had also grown steadfast in prayer, jubilant in worship and they had been tested in spiritual battle. But it was the strong contrary winds of opposition that tempered her growth. The antagonism came from three general sources: political, religious and tribal practices.

While Dean was still in Dilla, he was put under compound arrest by the governing Amhara. He was ordered to stay on the mission compound and could only go to the market by official permission. He was not allowed to travel into the surrounding district. The Amhara feared that any kind of help offered to the enemy Gadeo people would empower them. The mission was forbidden to educate them, which is why the Bible School was so small among the Gadeo. But the people were allowed to come to the compound. They came to Dean for training and discipleship. So even though he was confined, Dean's influence spread throughout the district and the church flourished under his watch.

The religious hostility was more sinister. The Amhara are primarily Greek Orthodox, dating back to the 4th Century A.D. when Christianity was introduced to Ethiopia. Hailie Selassie claimed to be a descendent of the Queen of Sheba and King Solomon. There is no definite historical proof of this, but the Amharic language is related to Hebrew, so there is some linguistic evidence to support their claim. The Ethiopian Orthodox Church also claims to hold the original Ark of the Covenant in a church in Axume, a town in Ethiopia. Each church is built after the pattern of the Jewish tabernacle, including both "holy" and "holy of holies" sanctuaries. Inside the inner sanctuary there is a replica of the Ark of the Covenant. They have their hierarchy of priests and all the teaching is done in Gheeze, which is a dead language that no one can understand. The services are filled with chanting and ancient rituals. All this to say, there is no reality of faith or relationship with the risen Christ. It is dead orthodoxy.

Many of the priests were corrupt. They used their positions to take advantage of the people. And they put up a lot of opposition to the followers of Christ. When a believer died, if he didn't own a piece of property, they wouldn't let him be buried on church or public land. The Orthodox Church was in cahoots with the government. A body could lie openly rotting for several days until somebody offered a place to properly bury it.

I recall an occasion when some local believers bought a piece of land to build a shop. An Orthodox priest went to the court to protest the purchase, claiming that he had already bought it. He had no proof of purchase, but he made the claim anyway. The judge was also corrupt, so he began playing the deal to see how much money he could get out of it. A dear friend got caught up in the scam. He was an older student in the Bible school. I showed him and the others the Scriptures that prohibit paying bribes. The judge promised he would decide on the case after the Christians had paid the bribe. He didn't call it a bribe, but that is what it was. So the believers would pay it and supposedly the priest would also pay some, but I doubt he was paying anything. They were probably splitting the profit. The judge would promise a hearing, but it was always postponed. Then he would demand another bribe. Every time the priest would supposedly give more money to the judge, he demanded more money from the Christians. This went on and on for over a year.

I advised the believers to stop paying the bribe and to trust God to make a righteous judgment. They sincerely surrendered the whole matter to Him and shortly afterward that wicked judge was removed and replaced by a just one. He reviewed the case and quickly decided in favor of the believers. They told me they then realized they never should have paid the bribe and should have trusted the Lord in the first place. In the end, righteousness triumphed over evil, but it came at a high price for those guys. It was a typical case of the injustices that led the unbelieving Gadeo people to ally themselves with the communists when they came into the country. Without the Lord and without the truth of His Word, they just went from being the victim of one lie to another lie.

Spiritual warfare was a constant reality in Ethiopia – for pagans, national believers and missionaries. We are all affected by demonic forces, because these powers are behind every individual or institution that opposes the will and purposes of God. The ugliest effects strike the people on a personal and tribal level. To minister in Ethiopia meant doing direct business with the devil and his demons.

My times of prayer with Howie were aimed at drawing closer to the Lord and also for drawing power from Him for service. Expanded ministry also meant more opposition in the demonic realm. Howie was more experienced, and he invited me to join him in an area where he was working south of Addis, where demons had a tight grip on the Gurage people. God had begun a powerful work there and Howie wanted me to help him train the new believers in some basic principles of spiritual growth. He considered casting out demons basic to spiritual growth. In this particular tribe, an occult practice had begun generations earlier in which every four-year-old girl was given a demonic guide during a ritual ceremony. The outcome was never good. The young girls grew up and went mad. They were hassled and threatened into doing the demon's bidding, hurting themselves and hurting or harassing others. By allowing one demon to enter, usually others followed.

Two women who had come to Christ were still being harassed by demons. The younger woman had sought relief from a Muslim imam in the area, but his chants and potions had no effect. She had also gone to the medicine man, but he had no power over the demons. When we entered her home, we simply prayed and sang worship songs and read Scripture aloud. The woman kept hearing voices inside her head, ordering her to do all kinds of horrible things. She was under great distress. Then Howie began to speak directly to the demons, commanding them to identify themselves. Speaking in a very low voice, they defiantly refused to give their names. But Howie persisted, demanding in the name of Jesus, by the authority of His shed blood, that they disclose their names. There were seven demons living in this woman, and finally they each spoke their name, each one the name of a local idol.

Howie commanded them to release and come out of the woman. Again, they refused. Howie read Scripture pertaining to the blood of Jesus Christ and asserted His authority over them. He asked the demons what sign they would give that they were going out of her. They said, "I will scream."

Then with loud shrieking and grotesque gyrations over the woman's body, the demons came out of her. As each demon left her, the woman spoke in her voice saying, "It has gone out."

Howie reassured the woman that she belonged to Christ and that when, not if, the demons returned, she must read the Scriptures he had read concerning the blood of Jesus. He stressed that this was her rightful authority and her only defense against them, but it would be enough to make them flee.

The next lady we visited looked like she was 90 years old, but she was probably only forty. Her son told us he had spent all of his money trying to find relief for her. The medicine man had taken his money, but he had given no relief. Howie repeated the same procedure: praying, singing and reading Scripture. It turned out that this woman had over a dozen demons driving her. At Howie's command in the name of Jesus, they all went out of her in the same manner that the demons had gone out of the other woman – with shrieks and gyrations.

I participated with Howie in all of this, joining him in prayer, singing and reading Scripture. I was learning from him. As I would discover, the believers in Dilla were also well practiced in demonic deliverances. I would also be learning from them as well.

12
Ethiopia in Distress

In the warm, wet climate at Dilla, it seemed that anything could grow. The soil there is fertile, a rich orange color, producing pineapples, pomegranates, oranges, grapefruit, passion fruit, guavas and mulberry bushes. Hibiscus and poinsettias grow higher than a house. And of course, coffee grows everywhere. But the political climate and landscape of Ethiopia was producing fear and turmoil. It was sometimes hard to believe that a country so beautiful and so bountiful could also be such a horrible place for people to live. The sinful hearts of men can ruin the choicest paradise.

When we moved to Dilla in 1975, I was thrilled to be starting over in what I considered an ideal situation for myself. I would be freed from a stationary Bible teaching role and released to travel among the churches in the district, identifying and discipling key leaders. But the situation in the countryside was far from ideal. It was getting desperate.

A horrific famine had struck Ethiopia following a five-year drought, particularly in the north. Thousands of people had starved to death and the corrupt Amhara-controlled government had made matters worse by hijacking foreign aid. Continuing food shortages and high unemployment led to a popular uprising against Emperor Selassie in 1974. The Marxists took full advantage of the situation. Selassie was imprisoned, where he died six months later in 1975. The Marxist dictator, Mengistu Haile Mariam, was viciously anti-God and anti-American.

With the country destabilized, tribal wars flared up across the country with thousands more dying. The Burji and the Guji people we had tried so hard to reach were now fighting and massacring each other. During the Marxist reign of Red Terror between 1976 and 1978, over a million Ethiopians died. Opponents to the revolution were sought and purged, killed without cause or trial. Nearly everyone was a potential opponent. Even children from age eight and on were considered a threat if they knew how to read and write, skills that help people to think on their own. Marxism is spread by propaganda and mind control. So education on our compound put the children in the school at risk. It also put our own children in danger, a day's drive away from us at Bingham Academy in Addis Ababa.

We were constantly living with the knowledge that our children were in harm's way. Jeanette and I prayed fervently for their protection. We also knew that the young churches in our area were in danger of being wiped out. Missionaries were fleeing the country and we were urged to follow. In a period of six months, 200 SIM missionaries left the country with only 30 remaining. Some were told to leave immediately with only the clothes on their back. But I kept sensing my work there was not yet done. I didn't know when or if it would ever be done, but I was sure I had still more to do. Perhaps just one more day's work, or maybe another year. Everything was uncertain and unpredictable. But the needs were ongoing and a sense of desperation permeated life. Through all the turmoil, God was patiently preparing His people to reap a bountiful harvest in Ethiopia. I believed He was keeping me there to prepare His laborers for the coming harvest.

Late in May of 1975, Jeanette and I fell ill with hepatitis. Marge Langford came daily to care for Joycie and to cook what little food we could eat. It was an awful sickness. Our urine was darker brown than our shoes. We both had yellow eyes and skin.

We were ordered to bed rest for three months. It was an order that was nearly impossible for me to follow. There was just too much to be done for me to lay in recovery. Some days I barely had strength enough to pray. In my weakness I often got discouraged. But in my groaning, the Lord was praying for me and strengthening me, and He was also empowering me to pray for Ethiopia. The country was even sicker than I.

In the early days of the revolution there were large and loud pro-Marxist demonstrations in the streets, especially in Addis. They marched with red flags flying with hammer and cycle. The poor were drawn into the uprising by the promise of land redistribution and free 22-acre allotments given to all. To those hopelessly oppressed people, a future and a hope sounded good. But they didn't see the hook under the bait. They didn't realize it would mean giving all their produce to the government. The land they would supposedly "own" would become the Marxist government's leash for controlling them.

I was still feeling weak when I headed out among the 123 Darassan churches to train and encourage leaders. In spite of the opposition, the churches rallied and in one month over 6,000 backslidden believers renewed their faith or decided for the first time to follow Christ. I kept urging them to encourage and strengthen the new and weak believers in view of the uncertain future. I had a strong sense that my job was to ensure that the church was ready for even tougher times to come. But with everything on the line, they were joyful. They gave out over a thousand Amharic Gideon Bibles. The Lord was obviously preparing their hearts for whatever might lie ahead.

In the remote region of Jum Jum, 30 churches had developed where believers had migrated. They were untaught and I wanted to get in there to train them. After getting the required government approval to hold two conferences, which had been very difficult during this tumultuous time, I stopped in at the police station to register. As they were finally allowing me to go, people from the community came and began to bring all kinds of accusations against me. "These people, they come in here and they stir up the people. This is what causes wars among us. They show movies." Well, that piqued the police officer's interest. He asked about these movies. In Addis Ababa, movies cost $5. He thought this movie was a great idea. A free movie! It was Easter weekend and I told him I would show the movie about the life, death and resurrection of Jesus Christ to anyone interested after our conference. Many in the end came to see it.

After leaving the police station, we moved out on a trail that no vehicle had likely been on since the 1930's when the Italians had built some roads in the area. Suddenly we bogged down in a swamp. Through the use of a jack and large rocks we were able to pull out of there late that night. Next we cut our way through a fallen tree and ran out of gas long before we should have. I put in more gas, but I knew at this rate we would not have enough for our return.

The next day we finally got to Jum Jum, a day late. In the evening, halfway through our meeting, it started raining. It rained and rained. It rained for two hours. So, everybody dispersed and went home. I really sensed that Satan was fighting against us as we sought to encourage these young believers.

Early in the morning I got up and went outside. It was raining. I just had to pray. "Lord, would you give me an answer for these conferences?" I got a big banana leaf, which worked as a good umbrella and found another to sit on. For two hours or more I prayed and waited on the Lord saying, "Lord, I am going to stay here until the sun comes out. You give me some kind of indication that it isn't going to rain any more on these conferences." Slowly, it started to break up. A little sun came out on the hills nearby. "No, Lord, it's gotta be right here on top of me before I take it that you really have answered this prayer." Finally the sun came out, shining brightly. "Thank you Lord, I believe you for this." It didn't rain during those conference meetings or the next conference.

On our descent from the first conference, we had gone only 20 km and I had already run out of five gallons of gas. I was losing gas fast. I talked with the leaders traveling with me. We had two options. We could send someone overland with two cans to get gas or we could ask the Lord to sustain our gas. We spent a half hour in serious prayer over this decision. As we finished, one of the leader's Bible dropped open and he began to read in Amharic, *"So we may boldly say: 'The LORD is my helper; I will not fear. What can man do to me?'"*[13] I responded, "That is God's answer for us. Thank you Lord. I believe you Lord, that you will take us out of here."

Traveling back to Dilla with extra gas cans attached

We showed the films and held the second conference. As soon as we finished, it bucketed. It poured for hours. The roads turned into mud. I had four chains for my jeep. Using chains requires more gas. We left with 40 miles to go. I put in my last can of gas. We were up in the highlands so I coasted whenever I could, all the way down to Wando, where I finally filled up with gas. When I returned home to Dilla, I checked to see what was wrong with my gas tank. There was a corroded hole, big enough to poke my finger through, in the bottom of the tank. The hole had been hidden under a strap. The Lord had sustained the needed gas as well as the needs of the conference. I didn't know how He had done it, but I knew only He had done it. We praised Him.

Another miracle happened when I got pulled over for having too many passengers. I was permitted to carry only four, and I had five. I went to the traffic department but they canceled my fine. It was another confirmation that the Lord was always with us and caring for us as we ventured out to serve Him. This was great for me to see, but perhaps even more for my ministry partner, Werku Golle. He was working with a German Wycliffe translator to translate the New Testament into the Darassa language. He was a good and faithful servant of the Lord, a gentle giant. He had a wonderful wife, Abebetch. She changed her name to Hallelujah after they were married. She was a very small lady with a huge heart for the Lord. I tried to take Werku wherever I went, knowing that everything he observed in me would make a lasting impression on him. He would need to carry the torch after I left Ethiopia.

While Ethiopians were being killed by the hundreds of thousands, the foreigners were mostly left alone. We knew they were opening our mail and reading it, so we requested that when people wrote, they use aerogrammes so that their letters would not be opened. We had to be careful about what we wrote home, sometimes using code words. Government-instigated rumors about us were flying all around. We were said to be working for the CIA, which gave rise to nationalizing our compound, as with other privately owned and church owned properties.

We also heard rumors of them bringing in a Russian or Chinese doctor to staff our hospital. I was actually hoping we would get one or the other because it would be wonderful to share the gospel and show the love of Christ to a communist doctor. But instead we received a young Ethiopian doctor named Tadeyos. He turned out to be a pleasant surprise – very kind and professional. He was also a believer! He was obviously there to help the people, not to aid the government. He was another of God's reminders that He hadn't forgotten about us in Dilla or His reason for placing us there.

As the turmoil increased across the land, students grew more reluctant to attend the Bible school. The national teachers also feared being implicated by teaching them, so we lost most of the teachers. The school dwindled from ten students to only five, and I needed to start teaching again. I taught five classes a day, but under those conditions I actually enjoyed teaching more than I had in Burji.

The Marxists were continually broadcasting threats and rumors over the radio. We never knew what to believe. But we did understand that to disobey or disrespect a Marxist order meant certain and sudden death. We heard of two students in Dilla who were shot and killed because they had made an unkind remark to a policeman. We often heard gunshots near and around our compound. When our school's students were told to go to a rally supporting the new government, we made sure they went. A rumor flew around saying that students who were beyond the fourth grade level would be required to teach reading and writing to the younger students. Boys above sixth grade would be conscripted into the army. We didn't know if any of this was true, but given the unpredictable rulings and killings by the government, we were ready for anything.

Communist gathering in Dilla

We were also ready to evacuate at a moment's notice. We kept a supply of food and emergency medicines – aspirin, eye salve, penicillin, anti-diarrhea, anti-malaria and other antibiotics — for the journey out of country, probably to Kenya. We knew the day was coming when we would need to go, but until that day came, I was determined to make the most of every opportunity because the days were truly evil. We were the last missionaries left in Dilla and among the last remaining in all of Ethiopia.

Sharing our favorite vacation spot with hippos at Lake Langano during uncertain times

At Bingham Academy, Melodie, Reenie, Shari and Debbie were among the last in their classes. Reenie had only one classmate left with her. The school compound was surrounded by a high wall, but they could hear shooting all around it. Reenie wrote about Melodie seeing two men lying dead, beheaded, on the way to church. Bodies were left lying in the open for days as a warning to anyone who had ideas of opposing the new rule. The kids lived with steady underlying tension. The teachers and dorm parents tried to stay strong and loving under the stress, but they grew anxious and irritable at times. When the shooting started up, the older kids steeled themselves to not show their feelings.

The younger ones couldn't conceal their fear. They curled up in a corner, huddled together and cried.

Most of the shooting in the streets happened at night. Reenie would stay up and count the shots – some nights more than a hundred shots were fired, not including machine gun fire. One night the communists shot seven men outside the school gate and left the bodies lying there for three days.

Melodie and Reenie stayed on the top floor of the dorm. They pushed dressers and wardrobes against the windows to protect themselves from stray bullets in the night. When the school alarm went off to alert the kids of a new outburst of gunfire, they would slide down the bannister two floors and then climb down a ladder to an underground hiding area. The last kid down was to pull a rug over the trap door leading into the crawl space. The kids remained perfectly quiet in that dark little space until the coast was clear again. Sometimes that didn't happen for several hours.

When word went out over the radio that the government was taking over all town and city properties, we knew our compound at Dilla, the Mission Headquarters in Addis and Bingham Academy now belonged to the communists. We were warned by SIM not to travel anywhere.

A government man came to see me at the compound. He informed me that they wanted to hold a big parade and celebration on our field. He also wanted to use our loudspeaker to blare out the communist propaganda speeches. All I could say was, "Ishe, Ishe," which means "Okay, Okay." I had no choice but to comply to keep the peace. I only asked that they keep from entering our private households. He promised me police protection, which he honored.

We heard that some believers in Burji were jailed for not signing a statement saying that hundreds had died there from the famine. The Marxists were using that tragedy and the Selassie regime's corruption to justify their takeover. But it was a lie, so the believers refused to sign it. And once again, the Lord used the jailed believers to spread the gospel among other prisoners.

We didn't know how long it would be before we were forced to leave the compound and relocate somewhere else, or perhaps be coerced to leave the country. Until then, we thanked God for each new day He gave us, while continuing to do all we could to serve the people. The local churches were given a nice plot of land with a spring and lots of coffee trees. I built a new house for us, made of cinder blocks, which was used by the teaching staff after we left the country.

A little deaf and mute boy kept coming to our door every few days. I offered him a little money, but he shook his head. He wanted something for his stomach. I gave him a piece of bread and he grabbed it and smiled happily. To me, he represented the plight and the need of a whole nation. Ethiopia wanted so much, but needed Jesus, the Bread of Life, more desperately than anything else.

13
A Shepherd Boy

During the spring of 1977, the urgency of the hour in Ethiopia put a pinch on all of our plans. Our SIM leaders advised us not to make ministry plans beyond a month ahead. Not knowing whether or not we would still be around at harvest time, we planted just a small garden. We started taking life a day at a time, which is actually how it comes to us anyway, so we were simply living realistically. But I was also concerned about the future of the Ethiopian church. I kept asking God to show me how I could help prepare the believers to endure the coming storm. He answered in a simple and beautiful way.

During one of my trips through the countryside, I heard a shepherd boy singing Scriptures while watching his cows in a field. I learned that he was a Christian and that he had listened to the Scriptures on a cassette recording which he had received from some other missionaries. He could not read, so he memorized the Scriptures by putting them into song. It was beautiful to hear God's Word ringing out through the valley. I immediately realized that this was the way the Lord wanted His Word to spread across the land. He wanted me to record the Scriptures so that the people could hear it, memorize it and even sing it in their own language long after we had left them.

I had no way of knowing then the significance of that shepherd boy's song for all of Ethiopia and beyond. It was the start of a vision later known as The Romans Project, a strategy for training pastors and church leaders, which came to me over 30 years later. The Romans Project has spread across Africa and into some other countries. It is now more refined than its humble beginnings, but it is still a simple strategy for getting God's people into the Word and for getting the Word into God's people. I have often seen that God's best work starts from very small beginnings.

Ethiopian shepherd boy

There were no recording studios in the Dilla area, so I jerry-rigged a soundproof room in our house. It was probably about the most primitive recording studio ever made, but it worked. I insulated the walls and ceiling with old mattresses, sleeping bags, pillows and blankets. I recruited a few literate national believers to read and record a few verses and sing some songs. The Ethiopians are wonderful singers and they love to chant and sing the Scriptures.

The idea soon spread among the church leaders and they urged me to provide them with as much recorded Scripture as we could, as soon as possible. They shared my sense of urgency. This led to months of work, proofreading Bible verses in both Amharic and Darassa. It also required arranging recording schedules and transporting the "voices" from the villages to our home. Those logistics were commonly interrupted by the rains and taking care of crops and family issues. It was hard to keep track of our best "chanter." He was the father of a large family and was a teacher at our Bible school, so he had many other demands on his time. He sometimes got distracted and I would have to go searching for him. Christians were constantly being harassed. Some were beaten in the marketplace and others were apprehended and imprisoned. So we were never sure what might have happened to him when he went missing for a time.

Our studio wasn't completely soundproof, so we needed to maintain total silence while we were recording. Sometimes in the middle of a recording the dog barked or the cat meowed. Other times Joycie cried or Jeanette dropped a pan in the kitchen. We would have to re-record. For every minute of successful recording, it took several hours of preparation and editing. It was a long, painstaking process, but we persisted. For all our simple methods and our outdated equipment, the recordings actually turned out very well. The people used simple, hand-cranked cassette players to listen to the recordings.

The Lord kept us in-country for more than a year beyond the time when we were first advised to plan for just a month in advance. After one year, we had recorded many major passages

Working on Scripture recordings in our home-made studio

and stories from the Old Testament. We had also begun recording the New Testament, and by early summer of 1978 we had finished the Gospel of Luke and Acts. The sound of believers singing God's Word by heart could be heard in many places. To me, it was the most beautiful sound on earth.

When I first began the Scripture recording project, I was intent on doing something that would simply outlast our efforts in Ethiopia. But as always, God made something simple into something beautiful, all in His time.

As long as the Lord enabled us to continue in Ethiopia, the best news we heard from home was that people were praying for us. Jeanette was a great letter-writer, although she had to carefully weigh what she told people in America, both about our work and about the situation in the nation. But she was always very clear about our desire for people to pray for us. She often simply wrote, PRAY! We both could sense the difference that prayer makes in facing spiritual warfare. We were also very grateful to have parents behind us who really prayed. In August of 1977 I wrote a lengthy letter addressed to both Jeanette's parents and mine. I have pulled some excerpts from it:

Dear Mom and Dad Hawkinson and Corey,

I have intended for some time to write to our praying parents to bring you up to date on how the Lord has been leading us and to explain why we are still here. I understand your concerns, and we greatly value your prayers for us during these days. We have felt carried on the wings of prayer.

As you know, during our furlough, we had definite assurance from the Lord that we were to return to Ethiopia. As it turned out, had we delayed our return until June, we would not have been allowed back into the country. So far, here at Dilla we have been spared many of the problems that others have experienced in other parts of the country. Perhaps our time will come to face the same troubles as other missionaries, but it appears we now have a living fence of angels surrounding us through which the Lord has permitted no intrusion from the enemy. We are indebted to the prayers of many for our current safety.

This past week we had the most encouraging conference with 215 elders from 120 churches. Each expressed a strong desire to learn more from God's Word. My heart welled up with praise to the Lord for His work in their hearts. All along I have been encouraging leaders to daily read from the Bible, but my words often fell on deaf ears until now. God is using this present trouble to move in the hearts of His people, starting with church leaders. I've often told them of the example I witnessed in my own father while I was growing up. Dad, I remember when you would come inside the house after working and the first thing you did was to sit on your chair and read your Bible and pray. You taught me to let the Lord form my thoughts based on His Word rather than from men or circumstances. My desire is to teach this vital practice to other men who will be able to teach others also.

I was invited to speak at a youth conference at Yerga Chaffe on August 4-7. I will preach four or five times. The expected crowd will be at least a thousand and it could easily be 2,000 on Sunday. There will be more conferences like this in the fall. It provides a tremendous opportunity to build into the lives of future leaders of the church here. I take it as further confirmation from the Lord that He wants us to be here for now. I feel complete peace about staying until He shows us otherwise.

One of the principles I plainly see in the Scriptures is the importance of expecting problems when you are walking in God's will and plan. A person could get very frustrated if he expected nothing but smooth sailing. But Jesus said we could expect trouble in following Him. He also said to wait on Him to work. I have not mastered this principle, but I am learning how to face the inevitable troubles that come while serving Him in this world.

I've been encouraged lately by the story of Elisha when he was surrounded by the armies of Syria. His servant was despondent. Then Elisha asked the Lord to open the servant's eyes to see the unseen realm of angels. When his eyes were opened, the servant saw things as they really are, from God's perspective.

The army of the Lord is always present and always greater than our enemies. As long as we are here in Ethiopia, God will give us the grace to bear up to the troubles we face if we are also facing Him. When He tells us it is time to go, we want to be close enough to Him to hear His voice.

Be assured of our prayers and love for you, and thank you again for your continued prayers and love.

Love,
John

I wrote that letter hoping to ease the concern of Jeanette's and my parents, but as parents ourselves, we understood their concerns. The war and the economic conditions in the country didn't bother me nearly as much as the thought of our children being endangered and exposed to the horrors of war. Reenie was a good little correspondent, but some of the news she reported really got to me. It was troubling to think of the long-term effects on them from living with such tensions day after day. She wrote in a letter from Bingham, saying that, while on their way to church in Addis, she saw a "red communist truck" carrying national kids who pointed black guns at them. Other Ethiopian kids roamed the streets carrying sticks and shouting pro-communist slogans.

One day Jeanette was walking with Shari, Debbie, Joycie and Shari's little friend to buy ice cream bars. As they came near the store, suddenly two soldiers started shooting at a man just twenty feet from them. The Lord gave Jeanette the presence of mind to duck into an alley, scurrying the children along with her. They were hiding in a parking lot when an Ethiopian woman motioned for them to move into the building stairwell. From there they heard gunshots being fired for some time in the lower part of the building. Shari's friend was crying uncontrollably, white as a sheet. Debbie was sure she'd been shot in the hand. She'd actually been struck by a pebble that had flicked up during the spray of bullets. They never did get their ice cream. The verse that so encouraged Jeanette at this time was Psalm 121: 7-8, *"The LORD will protect you from all evil; He will keep your soul. The LORD will guard your going out and your coming in from this time forth and forever."*[14]

On another occasion, Shari and Debbie were alone in their dorm with other girls, grades one through four, when shooting broke out around the school. The communists were chasing some nationals who tried to find safety at the school. Bullets were flying over the compound. Thankfully, a missionary dashed to the dorm to check on the girls and found them huddled together in a closet, crying their hearts out.

Shari wrote to tell us that she couldn't stop crying.

We didn't know where we might go as missionaries when it was time to leave Ethiopia, but we knew that day was coming, probably soon. Sudan was a possibility that was posed to us, and also Ghana. But wherever we might go, Jeanette and I figured on taking at least a yearlong furlough for the sake of our kids, as much as for ourselves.

The fighting in the northern part of the country was most intense between the Ethiopian soldiers and Somalia and Eritrea. When large numbers of Russian and Cuban troops and equipment entered the country and headed that way, we knew the war would come to a quick end. It was actually a relief to know the fighting and the killing was dropping, but it also ended the work of many of our missionary friends, including Howie Brandt.

Despite shortages of gasoline and certain foods, we continued to press on, trying hard to finish recording the Bible for the church we would soon be leaving behind. But even with the future of the country looking bleak, church leaders were beginning to plan for a better future. The leaders at Dilla decided to seek permission to purchase a piece of property, large enough to build a 600-seat building and with room to grow. I wasn't sure it was the best time for this, but they insisted on going ahead with the project. As with that shepherd boy I had heard singing the Scriptures, hearing their faith was truly music to my ears.

The Lord's leading is supernatural, but it is also practical. It was becoming more obvious that Bingham Academy would not likely be open for the next school year. There were just a handful of students remaining. Many of our friends in America were urging us to return "home." By then, Ethiopia was home to us, but we knew our time there was quickly coming to an end. We needed to get the girls back to the States so they could get situated for the coming school year there. I tried to stretch our time in Ethiopia up until the last moment possible so we could record more Scriptures. But a date for our departure was finally set for the last week of July.

We sold some of our belongings for small amounts. We gave most of our furniture to Werku and Hallelujah. They invited us to their home for a farewell meal. Their home was humble, but creatively decorated with newspapers lining the inside walls. The girls thought it was a pleasant place, much like Werku and Hallelujah themselves. We were sad to leave them, but I was glad to know that God had raised up such a fine man to whom I could hand over much of the ministry.

Werku and Hallelujah went around to each of us, washing our hands. This was an expression of honor and love. They made a special meal for us called Injera b' Wat, which is a delicious spicy

Hand washing in Werku and Hallelujah's home

stew eaten with sour flat bread.

There was no formal ceremony necessary for me to pass the mantle of leadership to Werku. It was already understood that he was God's man. He would be in charge of the Scripture recordings. I knew I could trust him to continue the work better than I. He was unwavering in the face of opposition and was later imprisoned for his faith. He refused to renounce Christ, and as a result was put in solitary confinement. He thanked the Lord for giving him the solitude he needed for finishing his translation work. It was there in a prison cell that he completed translating the Bible into Darassa.

Werku Golle recording Scripture

On our way back to America, our family stopped over in Israel. Jeanette and I had always wanted to go there, and this was our perfect opportunity. We camped under the stars by the Sea of Galilee. We visited Golgotha, where Christ was crucified. We saw the Garden Tomb where He is said to have been buried. I assigned the girls to research the Scriptures and report on every scene we visited. I wanted them to see that those were real places and that our faith in Jesus was based on historical fact. It was a great privilege for us to walk where Jesus had walked. It had been an even greater privilege that God would allow us to walk among His people in Ethiopia.

14
Wearing the British Flag

Coming back to America, we felt strange and out of place. Our kids were more African than American. Jeanette and I felt the same. It was hard to fit into the culture, even the Christian culture. It may have been difficult for people to understand us as well, but we appreciated all the expressions of kindness that were shown to us.

While growing up, my family was a regular recipient of the missionary barrel. I thought it was great when I found a pair of used shoes or trousers that fit me. So it was good news to me when I found that this practice of giving to missionaries still persisted, when I became one myself. One of our supporting churches, Emmanuel Bible Church in Seattle, had a "missionary cupboard" that was full of new sheets, blankets, towels and other useful items. It was a real treasure trove for Jeanette. Some of the ladies in the church, including Jeanette's mother, had formed a sewing group, and they liked to sew clothing for missionaries. They called themselves the "Dorcas Circle." Our kids and Jeanette wore some of the fine products of their kind and skillful hands.

A sewing group in another supporting church made clothing that was probably aimed at allowing for a child to grow into each article – a one-size-fits-all approach. Unfortunately, each dress hung like a sack on their bodies. The patterns were outdated and the fabrics and colors they chose sometimes clashed. That didn't really concern me, but the older girls, Melodie and Reenie, were very conscious of it, especially after they started school. Some kids made fun of them for wearing out-of-style clothes. It was hard for them to take. It was also hard not to take the things that were given to us, free of charge. I knew they were good-hearted, hard working people who had sacrificed their time, talent and treasure to help us do the Lord's work. But as we learned, sometimes well-intended giving is not done according to wisdom.

A missionary couple we knew in Ethiopia once received a package filled with used tea bags. A note was included in the box emphasizing that they had been used only once. The same thing happened with used soap bars that had been salvaged from motels. I always wondered why people couldn't send new tea bags and soap bars and use the recycled ones themselves. But I was thankful for anything that came to us. It was also easier to live out of the missionary barrel in Africa than it was in America.

In those days, we definitely fit the "missionary" image. But if our clothing was out-of-style, it didn't bother us because we weren't even aware, nor did we really care about styles until we came to America. Some might have thought, "Those poor missionaries are so out-of-it." But we didn't consider ourselves

Sporting our "style" walking home from church in Dilla

"poor" because we had seen how people in the rest of the world lived. It is when others see you as poor that you can start seeing yourself that way. As a missionary, being poor was even expected by some, as if it is more sacrificial and therefore more honorable to be poor. Our answer was just to live simply and to be ourselves, and we learned how to do that pretty well. We stretched every dollar given to us. Just as I had done growing up on the farm, I rarely discarded anything that might eventually be useful in some way – nuts, bolts, wire or any old piece of junk. I learned to jerry-rig vehicles and machinery to keep them running. I cannibalized car engines and running gear and I machined parts for fixing nearly anything that was broken.

When we took our trip to Israel, we flew from Ethiopia to Egypt, but due to political tensions between the two nations at that time, we could not fly directly from there to Israel. So we went first to Athens. I wouldn't dream of staying in a hotel, so we stuck our rope-tied boxes full of goods and clothing in storage and we camped on a sawdust pile under a tree in the Greek countryside, free-of-charge. We bought fresh fruit and street food, eating as cheaply as we could. We didn't eat in restaurants. I

Camping in Athens on a sawdust pile

was thankful for my poor upbringing because it taught me to value people who have few material possessions and to be grateful for what I have.

We stayed in a home in Bothell, Washington during that year while we were on furlough. Our neighborhood was a nice middle class community. We were low on funds, so I worked with my father-in-law in construction to make ends meet. It was a good year in many respects – being with family and friends again. Reenie, Shari and Debbie were baptized by my dad at a family reunion. Furlough was a much-needed break from the sights and sounds of war. But it was also a challenging year. The older girls went through hard culture shock in school. The American kids bullied others on the school bus, swore loudly and hung on each other inappropriately in the hallways. Some teachers poked fun at our kids' clothing in front of others. The girls had a hard time making friends except for among a few other social misfits. When people treat you like you are beneath them, it is hard for anyone to take. It was especially hard for our teenage girls. So it was good to see that Reenie was resourceful enough to tear out the seams of those baggy dresses and re-shape them into something nice. Sometimes the only fix that works is something nice, or better yet, something new. And we saw that God has ways of honoring His laborers that are both surprising and humbling.

I was seeking the Lord's leading regarding our next assignment, which boiled down to either Ghana or Liberia. Both are English-speaking countries. Knowing that I was not gifted in language-learning, I didn't want to learn another language and was mostly interested in joining a team involved in church-planting. Being still unclear about the Lord's direction, I received a letter in September from the SIM headquarters asking me to fill out a form that had been sent to them by a church in Knoxville, Tennessee that was seeking to expand its missionary involvement. I knew nothing about the church and was still unclear about the Lord's direction in my life. I figured they wouldn't know much about me either after filling out the form because I couldn't yet answer all of their questions. I just mailed the form and forgot about it.

Eight months later I got a letter from Cedar Springs Presbyterian Church in Knoxville, stating that they had decided to support us for $240 a month. To me, it was a clear confirmation that the Lord was calling us back home to Africa. So when that letter arrived, I read it aloud to the whole family and we rejoiced together.

I'm going to jump ahead in the story to tell how the Cedar Springs church blessed us even beyond their financial pledge, which they eventually increased to $800 per month. From the start they gave to us sight-unseen. When we finally did make it to Knoxville during our next furlough, we were apparently quite a sight to them, or at least I was. The church was holding their week-long mission conference and they gave each missionary a three-minute segment in the service to talk about their work. This was a church of at least 2,000 people, most of whom appeared to be upper-middle class folks. I had never been in a church that large. Most of our supporting churches ranged from 100 to 150 people. I wore the only sports jacket I owned – a red and blue plaid getup that was at least fifteen years old. The girls later teased that I looked like I was wearing the British flag. When I got up to speak, my jacket spoke louder than I did. I felt kind of conspicuous, but what could I do about it? It was the best I had to wear.

Jeanette and I met with the board of directors during the week. It was a

My British flag jacket

very august group. There were doctors and lawyers and big business men, each one dressed in dark, expensive-looking suits. I was full of trepidation, thinking, "Well, now that they'll be meeting the real me, straight from the bush, there goes all their backing." I was sure they would be totally unimpressed. But I was surprised at their genuine interest in us and in our work. They were so congenial and humble. Then one of the men took me aside and told me he wanted to take me downtown and buy me a new suit. He drove me to a specialty store where he let me pick out a suit of my own taste. I had no clue about the latest style but thankfully someone helped me. I knew I was suddenly in-style when I walked out of that store with that brand-new suit, perfectly fitted for me.

Someone in the church also took the girls to a room where they kept racks of new clothing. Apparently they had a connection with a clothing store or manufacturer. They told the girls they could take anything they wanted and all they wanted. Every article was the latest style and of the highest quality. The girls couldn't believe it. Jeanette and I were happy for them. It was all such a God-thing, and it was so good to see that He was showing them how much He cared for them and their needs. He had arranged for a church in Knoxville, Tennessee to partner with us in our work and to help provide for our needs. I had never even been to Tennessee prior to connecting with that church. And I could never have jerry-rigged or fit together a scheme like that.

Rather than simply appointing us to our next assignment, the SIM leadership allowed us to take plenty of time during our furlough to seek and pray about where we sensed the Lord was directing us. I appreciated their consideration. But after six months, I still had no clear sense of direction. Joycie continually pleaded, "Let's not go where there are any more guns this time." She still struggled with recurring nightmares in which guns were pointed at her.

I was torn between Ghana and Liberia, but I was leaning toward Ghana. That was where most of my displaced missionary colleagues from Ethiopia had gone, and that was where church-planting work was being done. SIM was not planting churches in Liberia at that time. That is what I felt the Lord had called me to do. But in Liberia, at the SIM radio station, ELWA, there was a school on the compound that went through eighth grade. After that, there was a mission-run high school in Bouake, Ivory Coast. Ghana had no school for missionary kids, so they all went away to Bouake. Now with five kids in school, that would have been costly. As we had often witnessed in Ethiopia, we knew the Lord is able to care for our children, but having gone through times of separation and turmoil there, our family was our primary concern as we were seeking His next assignment for us.

We continued praying but I still had no clear word from the Lord. So one day I told Jeanette I was going to write a letter to the SIM ministry in Ghana to inquire about going there. But as I sat trying to write that letter, I had no peace. I told Jeanette maybe I should write a letter to Liberia. So I wrote to them instead. Meanwhile, a notice from the post office had arrived for me at Jeanette's folks' home indicating that I had a package to be picked up. I let it go for about a month. It turned out to be a cassette tape recording inviting us to come to Ghana. But by the time I got it, it was too late. I had already gotten the ball rolling for us to go to Liberia. When I got a letter of acceptance to the mission in Liberia, I just thanked the Lord, not only for His provision, but also for His protection from letting me go in the wrong direction. Jeanette and I felt His peace in this decision.

It took longer than we had anticipated to get our visas. It took about six months, which was unusual. But even in that delay, God's timing was perfect. We needed to send Melodie ahead of us so that she could start high school on time in Bouake. Just the day before she left, Jeanette's mother had a heart attack and went to be with the Lord in heaven. We sent Melodie off the next day with another missionary family. We were all in tears and filled with grief as she went, but we realized that God had orchestrated that delay so that we could remain and help Jeanette's dad through his grief. This was another one of God's amazing gifts to us, delivered right on time and perfectly suited just for us.

15
A Restless Caged Lion

We arrived in Liberia in December of 1979, just before Christmas. The ELWA (Eternal Love Winning Africa) radio station compound, broadcasting Christian radio across western Africa, is beautifully set along the coastline with waving palm trees and warm water. The air there is steamy, and it hung like a hot wet towel on your face. In many ways it was ideal for raising a family –

Joycie, Debbie and a friend on the beautiful ELWA coastline

it was safe and clean, complete with a school and hospital almost in our own backyard. The best part was that, except for Melodie who was away at school in Ivory Coast, we were all together as a family.

Our peaceful life nearly crumbled four months later. During the night of April 12, 1980, Debbie woke up hearing shots ringing out in the distance. Melodie was at home from school and she groaned, "Oh, no, not again!" She voiced what was on all of our minds. We all feared it was a communist takeover, but it turned out to be a change of corrupt governments. A Liberian army sergeant, Samuel Doe, had seized power in a coup against President William Tolbert, becoming the nation's first president of non-American-Liberian descent. Liberia was established in 1847 by freed slaves from America. Through the years, their descendants ruthlessly ruled the local indigenous tribes, excluding them from political power and voting rights. Although Doe and his followers had brutally executed Tolbert, the coup won early support. After an imposed ten-day curfew, during which Tolbert's allies were hunted and killed, life returned to normal, at least for us at ELWA.

I was given a job title, Language Men Advisor, which basically meant I would be a spiritual mentor to the broadcast translators working there. It was a broad job description with plenty of room for my own interpretation and application – as long as it fit within the parameters and purpose of the mission.

For most SIM missionaries working at ELWA, that seemed to be sufficient. Sound engineers, radio technicians, teachers and hospital workers were right in their element. For the most part, it was a fine community of Christians working together and getting along with each other. But before long, I started getting uneasy. The compound was closing in on me. I felt like a caged lion. Hearing me sounding off, I think some people thought I felt it wasn't good enough for me there. But that wasn't it. It just wasn't big enough for me to do what God had put on my heart. Jeanette told me that in a prayer meeting a lady prayed, "Lord, help John Corey to settle down."

When God wants to grow our heart and our vision, He often puts us in places where we come to realize that we don't fit. He uses the discomfort we feel there to make us more patient and persevering, while also putting more pressure inside of us to move on to something else. Looking back, I think my unsettledness was the Lord's doing. It may not have looked or sounded like the Lord to others, but He was working in me, increasing my heart's desire to work for His good pleasure. He was giving me a greater vision for my life work. And I have observed that visionaries are generally very unsettled people. Thankfully, the Lord knew how to rightly interpret that dear lady's prayer. He didn't let me get settled at ELWA; instead He let me get more unsettled.

Before we came to Liberia, I had wanted to be involved in church planting. It was where my heart was all along. But ELWA was not a church-planting ministry. Neither the mission director nor the workers were motivated to plant churches in the area. The Monrovia area churches seemed to have that all covered. We attended an international church on the ELWA compound, but it didn't stir me much. I didn't hear anyone talking about reaching out in the area with the gospel. It pained me to feel so settled down.

I tried walking around in those ill-fitting shoes for as long as I could stand it, but I felt my heart crying out to the Lord for release from captivity. I started a study in Romans for hospital workers, but it was optional and only three or four attended, and it was usually a different three or four every week. I tried discipling some of the translators, but I felt they were only giving me lip-service when I tried to help them apply the truth to their lives. They seemed content to say all the right things to keep me off their backs.

As a part of my job description, I prepared and broadcasted daily devotional messages. I think they were probably useful to someone out there, but it was hard to say because you seldom hear any feedback from radio broadcasts. It took me three hours to prepare those ten-minute messages. Coming in at the heels of

Bill Thompson, a talented and popular broadcaster, I wasn't sure my messages were interesting enough, no matter how hard I tried.

I often drove the technicians to Bible conferences in towns where they recorded the messages for future broadcasts. I would sometimes sit there for four days and maybe get to stand up and give a two-minute greeting in token recognition for being an ELWA missionary. I started feeling like a wallflower.

It wasn't that I thought I was too good for that kind of service. It just wasn't what the Lord had put in my heart to do. It kept me feeling unsettled, but that is how God kept me seeking His will and plan for my life.

For a while I thought I had made a big mistake in coming to Liberia. I considered going back to Ethiopia. Despite the fact that there was a war going on there, I wrote to our mission leaders asking if I could return. They wrote back saying they weren't encouraging any missionaries to return, but they left it open to me to decide before the Lord. I didn't reply. I was hoping to get a more definite invitation to come, but I never heard from them again. I took that as a closed door.

I also wondered if I should have gone to Ghana after all. I wrote to the mission leaders there also. My good friend, Peter Jenkins, who had also served in Ethiopia, was working there now. I tried to meet with Howie Brandt when he was passing through Ivory Coast to get his thoughts on the matter, but I missed him. He had already gone back to Ghana by the time I got there. Then I got a letter from the mission in Ghana saying that it didn't seem the time was right for me to be there. So that door was also shut. That's when the Lord opened my heart to receive a burden that He was giving to me.

In the northern part of Liberia there was an unreached tribe called the Gbandi. We had a broadcast going there, but not with any apparent effect. Some Swedish Pentecostals had been trying to work among them, but with little results. There were three or four tiny churches, which really weren't actual churches – just outreach points. I had been praying for the Gbandi. The more I prayed for them, the greater my burden grew.

At that time Howard Dowdell was the new field director at ELWA. Until then, SIM wasn't doing much church planting in Liberia, but Howard was exceptionally driven, with a big heart for outreach into the country. So I went to him and expressed my burden. I suggested he put me with my friend Les Unruh, who was working in the Gola area. Howard told me he thought it would be better not to put two veteran missionaries together, but to assign some younger workers to go with them. I still had no particular place to go, but that same week we got an invitation from the Swedish Pentecostals to come to the Kolahun district in the north, to record a conference. Kolahun is the home of the Gbandi people. I asked Alfred Lumbay, a Gbandi translator, to come with me. He was glad to do it because he wanted some good material to put on the radio.

I wasn't too impressed by some of the antics that went on during the conference. Rather than grounding people in the Word, I thought the Pentecostals were just getting them all hyped up. I didn't hear anything worth recording. So I asked Alfred to take me around the district to scout out what the Lord had been doing there. I took a notepad along to write down all my observations. The Gbandi were divided between pagan and Muslim religions. I wanted to go first to the pagan areas, so he took me to a town called Polowu.

On the way there we met a man standing in the middle of the road. We pulled up beside him and asked about the town up ahead. He informed us that he had just moved there from Monrovia. His father had converted to Islam and he was still undecided. He didn't know whether to continue worshiping the spirits or to become a Muslim. I didn't say much more to him because he had to go, but that encounter left an impression on me. It gave me a picture of the spiritual plight of the people there. Until then, the only two choices they had were to follow the traditional tribal religions or Islam. Without the gospel being preached among the Gbandi, Islam was making fast gains, promising power to those who made the change. The man we met was still in the middle of the road, but it was probably only a matter of time before he would go one way or another.

I had been seeking the Lord's direction for three years – 18 months since we had moved to Liberia as well as our 18 months in the States. Thankfully He didn't leave me standing there in the middle once he had me on the right road. All the while I had been asking Him, "Lord, where are you leading me?" Until then, I didn't know the right way, but I recognized it when I finally saw it. I knew which way I should go, because He had already put it in my heart.

Alfred and I traveled to various towns and villages. We discovered that the Episcopalians were also present there, but only in a superficial way. They owned a lot of land and had employed some of the Gbandi. That seemed to be the draw to Christianity among the people. There were small gatherings here and there, and some people had a vague awareness of the Bible, but none that we encountered along the way had a clear understanding of the gospel. The Episcopal Church had allowed for a lot of syncretism, mixing biblical teaching with the tribal religion. But its influence on the people wasn't much better than Islam. Working through the tribal chiefs, the Muslims offered ruling power to those who signed up. The Episcopalian church offered jobs and profits to their converts. But nobody offered freedom to the spiritually oppressed. Only the gospel could do that for the Gbandi, and that was all I had to give them.

When we returned to ELWA, I submitted a report to Howard Dowdell concerning the spiritual condition of the Gbandi. He was enthusiastic about what I had experienced there. He told me I couldn't just leave them. I needed to return.

I couldn't stop talking about my experience there. I must have been very passionate, because many of the ELWA staff also got excited. One of the radio engineers, Don Walker, caught my vision and requested to be assigned with me to go and reach out to the Gbandi.

128

In February of 1981, Don and I took another trip to the
Gbandi district. Before we left, I asked the Lord to give me some
fruit among the people. I told Him this would be how I would
know He wanted me to move up there. When we came to a
village called Fassavolo, we asked if there was a church there. It
was a dusty village of about a thousand. Every house had a rusted
tin roof. Some of the men asked us to return in the evening and
they said they would collect a crowd of people. They also said
they had been wanting to speak with a missionary. When we
returned that evening, there were about 25 people gathered in
the town hall. The doors of the building were wide-open and
goats and sheep wandered in and out as they pleased.

Women pounding rice

I explained our purpose for coming to Fassavolo and I gave a
simple presentation of the gospel. Several men told us they
wanted to follow Christ. One of them was a man named Hena
Kpato. As a twin brother, he held a special status in the tribe
because twins are considered to have special spiritual powers. He

was also a Zoe, or a witch doctor, and he was deeply steeped in a secret tribal society.

Fassavolo

Hena later told me why he had recognized Jesus Christ as his Savior. About two months before we came to Fassavolo, he had been on his way to a secret gathering in the forest, when he was suddenly struck ill. He fell unconscious into a trancelike dream where he envisioned a stairway leading up to a beautiful city with concrete buildings. He climbed up and saw multitudes of God's people inside the city. He tried to go in, but someone prevented him, saying he wasn't yet permitted to enter. When he awoke he found himself lying in the dirt. His twin brother asked him what had happened to him, but he couldn't explain it. He only knew he wanted to go back there and find a way into the city. He tried for several weeks to visualize the city again, but his spiritual powers could not take him there. When I told the story of how Jesus had laid down His life so that people could come to the great Creator God, he immediately understood that Jesus was the only one with authority to let him enter into the beautiful city of heaven.

At the time I felt the Lord leading us to move up to Kolahun, I didn't yet know Hena's story. But I knew the Lord had answered my prayer, and that was very settling to me. In June we loaded up our Toyota four-wheel-drive vehicle and trailer with our younger girls, our cat, dog and chickens, and all of our household belongings and headed out on a ten-hour drive up the dusty, pot-holed, rutted road to Kolahun.

The mission rented a large building to house us and our headquarters. Some short-term missionaries joined us. The plan was for our kids to stay with us during the summer and then to return to their boarding schools during the school year. It would be the best of both worlds – stability for our kids and purpose for me in ministry. But as we would often be reminded, nothing in Africa was completely stable. Liberia was still recovering from the coup with a still uncertain future, just as I was settling down in the place of God's calling.

Traveling to Kolahun

16
Any Ol' Bush

One of the best pieces of advice I got when we first came to Liberia was not to tell people what I used to do in Ethiopia. Africa is a big and varied continent, and what works in one country doesn't always translate to the next. Of course, it didn't take me long to realize the truth of this counsel. Liberia is a long way from Ethiopia in a lot of ways. The most obvious difference is the language, but the people differ in appearance as well. Ethiopians have sharper facial features and Liberian faces are usually more smooth-edged. The customs and food are also quite different. But one thing every nation has in common is sin, rebellion against God. The solution to that problem is always the same.

Despite the obvious differences between the two nations, it was hard not to make comparisons. Thankfully I had learned an important lesson in Ethiopia: if you don't know what you're doing, don't pretend to be an expert. Be a learner. Be a student of the people you are there to serve. And let the Lord teach you how to build His church. I sensed the Lord leading me to plant churches among the Gbandi people, but I had never planted a church before. That became both a hindrance and a help. Had I been a church-planter in Ethiopia, I might have had the urge to try doing it the same way in Liberia. The needs were blatantly obvious, but so were my deficiencies.

In Ethiopia I had worked mostly with established churches. I focused on discipling key leaders there. I was not an evangelist, nor did I need to be one. The Ethiopian evangelists were very effective. But to be a church-planter in Liberia, I also needed to be an evangelist.

As I had seen many times in my life and ministry, this is God's formula for success: my weakness, His strength. If He could speak to Moses through a burning bush, He could speak through me, as long as my heart was aflame for Him. With God, any old bush will do. Bushes grow in ordinary, obscure places. So God took an ordinary person like me and put me in an obscure place.

Soon after we had moved into our home in Kolahun, people started coming around the house to see us. They started studying us before I had a chance to study them. And they took long, close looks, peering through our windows with their noses pressed against the glass. Sometimes twenty to thirty children, women and men were looking in at us to see what they could see. We lived in a fish bowl. It was a little disturbing to be watched all the time. When the girls ventured outside, people swarmed around them, stroking their hair and touching their white skin. Some people wanted to talk about the gospel, and I thought it was great. Within a couple weeks I had started Bible studies for them. They were praying and asking the Lord into their hearts. They were agreeing with everything I was teaching. I thought, "No wonder the Lord called me here. It is such a fruitful place." I was starting to think maybe I was an evangelist after all.

Then they started asking other questions: "Do you have a job for me? I have this problem; could you help me? I need some money." It took a while to click with me. But when they stopped coming to the Bible studies after I had told them I couldn't help them out, it became all too clear. It was all for personal gain. It didn't take long for me to see that things were not as they seemed. I could see that I had a lot yet to learn about the people the Lord had sent me to serve.

I had been reading about how some missionaries had entered certain cultures around the world and had found a tribal "key" that had opened the way for the gospel to come in. Before we came to Kolahun, I had looked for some of those cultural keys. When Don and I were on our scouting mission, we visited a village called Bakanda. We told the people we had come to introduce them to the Savior of the world. They said they already had a savior of their own. The story went like this:

In the early 1900's the Mandingo people from Guinea, speaking Maninka, were raiding in the north of Liberia and they were sending war parties into the Gbandi area of Liberia. The local witch doctors came together to discuss how they could stop the invasion. One of their higher-ups said they would need a voluntary human sacrifice to come forward and die for the people. When the situation was looking desperate, a young Gbandi tribesman finally stepped forward to be martyred for his tribesmen. It was agreed that he must be shot with seven arrows. After eating his last meal he was pierced by seven arrows, but he didn't die. So they buried him alive. They stuck a bamboo shoot into his grave so he could keep breathing, and he lasted seven more days until he breathed his last. To the Gbandi, this was a miracle. And the invasion never came, which they considered another miracle. The martyr's grave is in Bakanda and it became a holy shrine. The people made annual sacrifices to him there.

I thought this might be the "key" I was looking for. I tried to explain to them that Christ was God's sacrifice for the whole world, but that didn't matter to them. It was more significant to them to have a local martyr, a savior from among their own people.

I don't doubt that God has given discernment to some missionaries in finding such cultural keys for unlocking people's understanding of the gospel, but He never gave me those kinds of insights. I knew I needed to be sensitive to the unique cultural features of the Gbandi, but I stopped looking for a special "key" to open up their understanding of Christ. I knew that love can open a closed heart, and the cross is the master key to every person's heart. It is essentially sin, not culture, which keeps people from coming to God. Apart from Christ, every person is bound by sin.

Ultimately, it is His business to see that people come to Him. I just needed to be faithful in love and faithful to the truth.

But like all cultures, I found that the Gbandi were entangled by unique strains of sin. Rather than looking for a special key to help them understand the gospel, I looked instead for where the people were bound. As an ambassador for Christ, it was my job to speak the truth in love concerning those strongholds. I often felt weak and frustrated at the few and slow responses I saw, but my confidence was not in myself, but in the power of God's Word to do the talking.

Sharing God's Word with people in a village

Like the jungle that surrounded Kolahun, Liberia was a tangle of sin from top to bottom, both culturally and personally. As in other African countries, parents traditionally had arranged the marriages of their children by a system of dowries. It could be a corrupt and heartless system, but it did keep sexual sins from running rampant. It accounted for some societal stability. But after the coup, the government did away with the dowry system to protect young girls from being sold into marriage to old men. It seemed like a humane response to such an injustice, but nobody bothered to instruct parents in how else to find a mate for their sons and daughters. So they just let nature take its course. By the time their daughters had reached puberty, a parent would tell her, it's time you went and found a man. The boys got the same shove for finding a wife. They did what came natural to them. Promiscuity became the acceptable norm. I'd say it was nearly 100 percent in Liberia. Probably 90 percent of the young people lived together unmarried. Even those who were trying to follow Christ were weighed down by that sin. It kept pulling them back and keeping them bound. Sexual temptation was everywhere and it never let up. It was all in the open.

But the Gbandi also had their secrets. There are secret societies among them called "devil bush." Before education and westernization, these societies provided structure and kept tradition alive among the tribes. Boys entering puberty would be sent out to the bush for up to three years to learn a trade and to learn how to be a man. They also went through secret rites of passage that introduced them to their spirit guides. The initiation was done by a "devil," a masked witch doctor dressed like a devil and often standing on tall stilts. Those being initiated had their faces painted eerily white. The girls had similar initiations. There were secret handshakes that revealed both belonging and status in the group. The devil bush societies were built around a sophisticated hierarchy. When formal education was introduced, tribal life skills were no longer stressed. This reduced the time that kids spent away from their families to just a few months in the bush, but they still got a spirit guide.

Every now and then, the "devil" would come to town. A town herald would cry out, "The devil is coming!" The initiated would run and join him, dancing and shouting as they went. The uninitiated would run for cover, hiding behind closed doors and shuttered glassless windows. To look upon the devil with uninitiated eyes was said to mean certain death. I don't know if any uninitiated person ever died just by looking at the devil, but some might have been frightened to death by the sight of him. In any case, they believed they could die, so in their minds it was true. We weren't afraid of the "devil," remembering what God said, *"You are not to fear what they fear or be in dread of it. The LORD of hosts shall be your fear, and He shall be your dread,"[15]* But we kept behind closed doors when he came to town. We recognized that it was all purely demonic and it kept the people bound by fear.

As I said, the only "key" I had and the only one I counted on was God's Word. The gospel sets people free. But not always immediately. Lasting fruit comes after years of labor. The "fruit" that I saw spring up during those first few weeks of our time in Kolahun didn't last. There were some exceptions, such as Hena. But most fell away. Eventually we started a Bible school, which we referred to as the Discipleship Training Center. It wasn't an in-depth program, but it offered a start for those who wanted to learn about the Lord. Some of the students seemed to be growing in the knowledge of the Lord, but none really stood out with great passion for Him. From among them, we sent "leaders" out to the villages to instruct others in the truth, but it didn't seem to take deep root anywhere. I could sense that something was missing, but I couldn't put my finger on what it was.

I rode my motorcycle to check on the work in the villages. The road was very bad near the town of Fassavolo, so I offered to get it fixed. We hired a contractor to come in and grade it. The operator of the road-grader was from another tribe. He was making good progress when he was alerted that the bush devil was coming. He stopped working and ran off. When I got to the village, the people were irate with me for hiring a person from another tribe. I hadn't hired him myself, but I couldn't explain that to them. I just apologized for it and asked for forgiveness. One of the leaders knew I was not at fault, so he asked me why I asked forgiveness for something I hadn't done. I told him it was wrong according to their understanding, so I was only asking them to forgive me from their point of view. I didn't need to be understood. I needed to understand. Later we had a group meeting and there was an amazing reconciliation.

This was an important lesson for me to learn as much as it was for the people to see. I didn't need to know all the reasons behind every problem, nor the secrets of every heart. I needed to be faithful in love and faithful to the truth. That was the key the Lord had entrusted to me.

17
The God Man

One of the most important realizations Western missionaries in Africa must come to, is that we think differently from the people we are trying to instruct in the good news of Jesus. One difference is called linear versus circular thinking. Every culture has a mixture of both kinds of thought processes, but each seems to lean primarily in one way or the other. Neither is wrong; they are just different. Linear thinkers such as myself come to the mission field and make plans and set goals and measure progress by imposing our own timelines on the Lord and upon the people, only to see our best-laid plans and schemes fall apart sooner or later. Africans see the world as a constantly unfolding story that is guided by many conflicting forces. In the African mind, time doesn't decide the way the story goes. It only introduces new occasions that help the story to move along.

This observation is basic to understanding the people on a spiritual level. In the Western world, we tend to explain things in scientific, naturalistic terms. This is true even among Christians. We just don't realize how much we have been influenced by our rationalistic educational systems. And so we think in terms of facts and figures, causes and effects – factors that lay things out in nice straight lines and which we consider essential for knowing "truth." These are all elements of truth, but not necessarily the whole truth. Africans see a spiritual cause behind every happening. They may not be able to explain it in sound scientific or logical terms, but that doesn't mean they're entirely ignorant of the truth. I discovered it was far too easy to sell them short on what they understood and therefore miss out on the lessons they had to teach me about trusting the Lord.

Hena was one of my best teachers. He had been a witch doctor and he was well-acquainted with the spirit world. After he became a follower of Christ, he still struggled to let go of some of his occult practices. He had made a decent living from it and he had enjoyed the prestige it gave him in the village. Not letting go of these things was keeping him from growing in the Lord.

Bible study with Hena

I often spoke spiritual truths in story form, so I told Hena a simple little story: "A man was standing in two canoes, one foot in each, floating down a river. What do you think happened to him?"

Hena didn't hesitate to answer. "He fell into the water."

"Why couldn't he stay in both canoes?" I asked him.

"The two canoes spread apart because a canoe cannot support only one leg," he replied. "Both legs must be standing inside of one canoe."

"What will happen to the man who keeps trying to stand in two canoes?" I asked him.

"He will keep falling," Hena replied.

"Hena," I said, "you are that man!"

Hena understood my point. He burned his fetishes and threw away his magic potions. From that point on, he began to see God do amazing miracles in answer to his prayers. But he wasn't really amazed by the miraculous.

Hena was a head man in his village, which was surrounded by a thick forest. Rice is the staple food in Liberia. There are at least 25 different varieties. The Liberians only have a few words for various color combinations, but they have many ways of describing rice.

Every year farmers cleared new rice farms from the forest. Trees grow so quickly in the tropical climate, that every eight years they needed to be cut down again to farm the land. Some trees grow up to a foot and a half in diameter in that short time.

The farmers whack and slice the trees with a machete until they fall. Then they pull together piles of wood and let it dry for a few weeks before the rainy season begins. If it comes too soon, they can't burn the fallen trees and so they won't have a clear space for planting rice. Farming is a matter of timing, but not according to a clock. To Hena, timing and the weather, planting and harvest, were all matters that were under God's control. One year he decided to expand his farm by several acres so that he could plant more rice.

After he had burned the big woodpiles, Hena and his family prepared the soil around the stumps, bending their backs all day long while chopping deeply into the ground with a short hoe. It was grueling work, but they worked at it steadily until it was all done. This method aerated the soil. Then they did the "scratching"—hoeing the soil on its surface and sowing rice seed.

Burning trees and brush to plant a rice farm

After the seed had been planted, hundreds of birds swarmed above the farm and flew down to snatch it up from the soil. Hena's family criss-crossed strings with tin cans tied to them over the farm. When the birds swooped in, the kids pulled the strings, clanging the cans; they also threw rocks and shouted at the birds. It was an ongoing battle, but Hena and every farmer knew it was just a part of life. He knew the birds of the air needed food too, and since he understood that it is God who feeds them, he figured this was one of His ways of caring for them. As a farmer, Hena was just one among many conflicting forces in the bigger story that they all were living in.

After the shoots had sprouted, the groundhogs and porcupines would come into the farms and chew off the stalks and devastate the crop. Normally Hena would be prepared for this invasion. He would build a two-foot high stick fence that slanted outward at an angle. This barrier around his farm would keep most of the varmints from invading. Farming required constant vigilance.

But this particular year he didn't have time to do all of that. He was too busy walking out to all the surrounding villages and telling the people about Jesus. So he entrusted his crop to God for His protection. He prayed, asking Him to watch over his farm, and then he left it in His hands. Hena's faith was both simple and solid. He firmly believed that God would take care of his crop. And he was not even surprised when the birds flew right over his farm to a neighbor's farm where they had their fill. The neighbor was not a believer.

When he asked Hena why the birds and the animals didn't invade Hena's farm, even though he hadn't completed the fence, Hena laughed and told the man it was because he trusted in the living God. He acted startled that the man didn't understand this. The neighbor told Hena that he too would ask God to protect his farm. But he didn't want to follow Christ alone. He would only ask Him to protect his farm. He also placed ju-ju charms on sticks all around his farm to catch the evil spirits. Hena laughed as the man went his way.

He also laughed as he watched the man chasing birds from his farm every morning and evening. Following Hena's example, the man did not make a stick fence to keep out the animals, and the groundhogs and the porcupines feasted on his crop. It was comical to Hena. The man wanted God's favor apart from His Son. It may seem cruel of Hena to mock his neighbor's misfortune, but to Hena it was a teachable moment for his neighbor to acknowledge the power of Jesus Christ. He wanted him to realize the truth of the gospel by the power in His name.

One day Hena noticed that an animal had cut a swath at the edge of his farm. He was shocked by this. He had been certain that God would protect his crop. But just a few steps away he found a dead groundhog. Then Hena rejoiced because God had also provided meat for his wife to cook with their rice meal.

On the east end of Hena's village there was a sacred worship area where only women could go, in the center of which was a great big bay tree. It branched out broadly in five directions. The women of the village worshiped that tree, as had their ancestors.

Being an animistic culture, it was one of their many gods. One day they were having a worship feast. As they were drinking and dancing and shouting around the tree, Hena was sitting on a bench outside his house reading his Bible. The women came near him and started mocking him, shouting, "Hena, why do you worship the white man's god?"

Hena interrupted them and shouted back, "You shouldn't be worshiping that tree! I worship the God who made that tree and He can make it fall down!"

The women started laughing, saying it could not fall down. It had stood for centuries through the fiercest storms. For three days they taunted Hena while chanting all the louder, giving homage to the tree. They sang antiphonal songs, making merry while hallowing the tree and mocking Hena and his god. That really vexed Hena. Finally he said to them, "Tomorrow you shall see! God will make that tree fall down!"

Hena went inside his house and fell on his knees before God. He said to Him, "Have I said too much? I ask you to make that tree fall down so they will know that You alone are God."

The next morning came with clear and very still skies. It was a perfect day for a storm. In the afternoon a thunderhead formed over the village and a sudden squall burst into terrific winds. Tin roofs went flying everywhere. The big bay tree swayed and twisted and finally exploded. Only one large scraggly branch remained. Huge broken branches were scattered everywhere. The top section of the tree landed near an open kitchen where people were standing when the wind had picked up. But it landed safely near them and no one was hurt. Many villagers started shouting, "Hena's god is strong! Hena's god is strong!"

The women were very angry at Hena for destroying their god, so they went to the village chief and demanded that he force Hena to repay them for their loss. He asked them if Hena had directly caused the tree to be damaged. They said he had not. He asked them if anyone had been hurt by the fallen tree. They assured him that no one had been injured. "Then take it up with Hena's god," he pronounced. He dismissed the case. I am not sure if any of the people turned to Christ for salvation due to that display of His power, but it did make a definite impression on them. From then on, they called Hena "the god man."

Hena's faith also made a definite impression on me and on our family. When we saw how God answered his prayers with such power, we were encouraged to pray in the same way. As time progressed it started to become a normal part of our lives to ask the Lord to act and then to wait expectantly for Him to answer.

When we first moved to Kolahun, we rented a large house. It had a big metal drum beneath the eaves of the roof for catching rainwater. That was the purest supply of water available to us. The rivers in the area were swimming with leeches and parasitic worms called schistosomes, which cause a painful disease of the urinary tract and the intestines. There was a well down by a stream near us, but its water was filled with a reddish, goopy algae. It was not fit to drink. Our only good source of water came from the sky during the rainy season. A big downpour could fill the drum in a short while. It usually took a couple weeks for it to run low again. But it often got down to just an inch or two of remaining water, so then we scrimped on water usage, only using it for drinking or cooking. We learned to bathe using just a bucketful of water. When the water got really low, we sometimes went for two weeks without a bath at all. In a hot climate, that was rather unpleasant. We prayed together quite often for God to bring rain. One time when we were in dire need of water, Jeanette and I gathered the girls and we prayed. As we prayed it started to pour, replenishing our drinking water.

To this day, each of our girls has a strong faith that God answers prayer. When the rain finally came, it usually came in torrents. The weather was always warm, so the girls could run outside and stand under a waterfall running off the roof, washing their hair and showering fully clothed in the warm water. Here in America, we just step inside a hot shower in the mornings and think nothing of it. But in Liberia, the girls knew that every one of those showers was a gift from God. After two weeks of going without a bath, it always felt like a miracle, even if it wasn't. We learned that miracles are as natural to God as they were to Hena.

While I still had the sense that there was something holding most believers back from fully trusting the Lord, He also used Hena to free me from some holdups in my own heart. Hena's simple faith reminded me of my father's. I had always wanted to trust God in the way that he had leaned on Him, and now He was using Hena to teach me how.

Along the way to a town called Samolahun, a lady named Ma Korpu had a farm. She was a lovely believer. She was also a lead singer in her church and she joyfully told others in her town about the Lord. I often stopped there while riding my motorcycle to Samolahun. Ma Korpu's husband was the mayor of Kolahun. He was older so he couldn't help much around the place. She complained to me that the birds and the animals were ruining her farm. I remembered Hena's prayer, and so I told her, "God says He feeds the birds of the air and the animals, so let's just ask Him to feed them somewhere else."

We prayed together, asking God to protect her farm from all the destruction the birds and animals were causing. Sometime

Women leading music while walking to a baptism

later I stopped by again and I asked her how her crops were doing. She said the birds and the animals had stopped coming there. I think my look of surprise was sufficiently concealed by my genuine joy. She probably assumed it had come as simple for me to ask God to do this as it had come to Hena.

18
A Brush With Faith

When we were in Liberia, half of the children born there didn't live to the age of five. Perhaps that statistic has since improved, but it was a frightening reality then. As Jeanette and I knew from our own experience in losing Nathan, it is every parent's fear. It was a fear that most Liberian parents had to live through. It created an atmosphere of dread and fatalism. Infant death was so prevalent that people went numb to the pain of it. Children who died before age five weren't even given funerals. Little children weren't given meat for their rice because they might not live anyway. If it was their fate to get sick and die like so many other children, it would have been a waste to feed them the nutritious food. We often saw little children crawling beneath a table scavenging for scraps that had fallen while the older children and adults were eating.

There is a cause behind every disease that takes a child's life. The tribal people believed there was a spiritual reason behind it all. They thought someone might be angry with the family and had cast a curse on them. Or maybe one god was jealous because a greater sacrifice had been given to another god. Who knows? Fear, confusion and uncertainty are the means Satan uses to control people, making it impossible for parents to know why their children had died. All they knew was that it was somehow related to the spirit-world. And they lived in dread that death was bound to take one or more of their children.

Liberian mothers also have a practice of "stuffing babies" with rice gruel to fatten their malnourished little bodies. Holding their noses tightly shut, they would pour the mixture into their little mouths. Unable to swallow it, the babies sometimes died from choking. It was only natural to their mother-hearts to aid their baby's growth. So it was hard to persuade them that this was a potentially deadly practice, because their own mothers also had fed them in the same way.

The truth is that most of the diseases that take the lives of children are preventable. They are traceable to poor sanitation habits. The village people didn't have toilets, so they relieved themselves out among the coffee trees, and when the rains came, it all washed into the water and contaminated it. This is an example of when linear-thinking is helpful. It helps you draw a straight line from the poop to the problem. We would call it common sense, but it is also a cultural awareness that we in the

Children under five often had only plain rice
with little nutrients.

West possess.

SIM recruited nurses to treat the sick and to help people understand the causes of the diseases causing death. They taught mothers to squeeze an orange, adding some water and salt to balance their electrolytes. They also gave out antibiotics that saved children's lives. In this case, our Western ways were right. But more importantly, the truth was being dispensed in love. Only love can cast out fear, but fear never lets its captives go without a fight.

Hena told me that when he was a Zoe, a medicine man, the people's fears played right into his hands. One day a distraught mother brought her sick child to him for help. He used a divination practice called sand-cutting in which he poked holes in a pile of sand with a stick, determining a pattern which he claimed guided him to diagnose an illness and prescribe its remedy. He had all kinds of magic herbs, roots and mineral potions on hand to sell her. He told me this was just one story among many others like it. But this lady seemed to have more money than others and her child was near death. He knew he could bilk her for more than usual. He told the woman he had never seen such a hard case. It would take a pan of rice, a jug of palm oil, a chicken and five Liberian dollars for him to make it work.

The lady went home and retrieved all he had demanded. Hena did his sand-cutting again and then told her there was actually more to the problem than he had previously realized. "It's your grandmother," he said. "She is very angry at you because you have not sacrificed to her lately." Her grandmother was dead, and it was true that she hadn't sacrificed to her lately. She believed her grandmother's spirit could still haunt her. Hena told her the grandmother had cast a curse on the child. He said, unless she made a sacrifice to her, her child would die. She would need a very powerful Zoe to break the spell.

In her fearful state, the mother went right along with his ploy. "You are the one who found the problem," she insisted. "You must know the way to break the spell."

He told her it was much too difficult of a case for him to solve. But she insisted that he must try. He kept insisting that it was a very hard case, and the mother kept begging him to carry on. Finally he relented. He said he would need three pans of rice, two jugs of palm oil and another chicken. He said she should also bring fifteen more dollars. She was startled at the cost. Sensing she might back out of it, Hena told her, "Just bring me half of it, and when the child has recovered you can bring me the rest."

The woman brought to Hena all he had asked of her. He sacrificed the chicken for her and then she left. He ate the chicken.

Soon afterward Hena's wife, Hawa, came home and said to him, "Have you heard? The lady who came to you – her child has died."

Hena handed his wife a coin worth about 25 cents. "Take this to her and comfort her with it," he said.

Hena left his village for a few days after that. He told me, "What I was doing was a total lie and I knew it. It is what all the Zoes did."

He also knew that there were lying spirits behind his occult practice that were keeping the people bound by fear and confusion. And while the people were playing into his hands, he too was playing into the hands of the devil. When Hena came to know Christ, he understood that God is in control of every power in heaven and on earth. He began to pray with a new power that was controlled by love.

One day I went to Hena's village, Fassavolo, to have a Bible study with him and some other guys. Before we started, he brought a young lady to me and said, "This is my niece." She was maybe twenty years old and she had a small child. She was his twin brother, Sillay's, granddaughter. Sillay had brought her up from Monrovia to see Hena because she was demon-possessed. His brother was not a believer, but he realized that Hena had a very strong spiritual power over the demons.

The spirits kept harassing the girl day and night. Before she came into the room for the Bible study, she had run off into the village and it took eight men to haul her back, kicking and screaming. The room was half as large as my whole house and it was packed with people. Sillay had eight wives and lots of children.

Hena's niece was cowering in a corner. She grabbed a stick and started shouting, "I'm going to kill all of you!" All the girls fled the room. The older ladies stayed. I wasn't sure what I was facing. I didn't yet know if she was just crazy or if she had a demon. So I prayed, "Lord, give me discernment and wisdom to know what to do."

She said she wanted to go outside to relieve herself, but the women told her she couldn't leave, suspecting she would not return. She kept inching toward the door where I was standing. I put up my hand and nicely said, "No." She barely brushed my finger and then she jumped back.

"Your spirit is too strong for me," she said. She backed up and sat down. Then I knew she had a demon, perhaps many. I told Hena we should go into another room where there weren't so many people and have our Bible study. When we were done, I asked about the young lady. She was outside feeding her child and she seemed very calm. When she had finished, one of the women invited her to come back inside.

We sat in a hallway and I began explaining the gospel to her. She was still calm and she seemed to be following my explanation. It was an easy conversation. I asked her why she had threatened us with the stick. She told me the demons made her feel very frightened. She said they were always telling her she would die if she ate a certain food or wore a certain article of clothing. They would also tell her if she lay down in a certain spot she would die. Everything she did seemed to carry a threat of death.

We continued to talk and before long she prayed and received Christ into her heart. But she was still very fidgety. Whenever anyone walked into the room she got so nervous she wanted to leave. I told Hena we should go over to his house where there wouldn't be any distractions.

At Hena's home, I read to her some passages from the Scripture concerning Christ's power and authority over her and the whole world. She started trembling and shaking, so I knew there were demons trying to regain control over her. She had a terrified look in her eyes. Hena joined me in praying over her, claiming the authority of the shed blood of Jesus on her behalf. We began singing hymns and praising God together. We rebuked the demons and told them they had to leave her. Again, she yielded her will to Christ. A visible calm came over her.

She was somewhat educated, so I gave her a Bible to read. Her child had been playing outside while we were inside praying. Through an open window we saw the child get bumped by another child. She immediately sprang up and shouted, "Are you trying to kill my child?" I could see that fear still had a grip on her. I didn't say anything about her overreaction, but I told her she needed to begin filling her mind with God's Word. I gave her some passages to read.

A few days later I went to Hena's home and he told me that he too had been advising his niece. "I warned her that the demons would return and try to make her afraid again," he said. "But she needs to resist them in the name of Christ and in the power of the blood of the Lamb. I told her to tell them that she belongs to Christ now and they have no part of her."

That night when she lay down to sleep, she put the Bible under her toes for protection. She awoke and felt the heavy sense of the demons coming over her, so she reached down and grabbed her Bible. It was too dark for her to read it, so she just held it close to her heart. The demons left her.

When I saw her again, I encouraged her more in the Word. She seemed completely normal. The look on her face was peaceful. I explained to her how to cast the demons away from her if and when they returned. She seemed to understand. But a few days later something happened that set her off again. In the marketplace she saw a woman who recently had been operated on and her sutures had come apart, exposing an open sore. The sight of that caused her to start screaming in horror. It triggered her fear of dying. The demons suddenly took hold of her and she fled into the forest. It took several hours to find her and bring her back. Hena sat with her and calmed her down.

She was back to normal again when I came to speak with her. I told her, "Satan was using fear to control you. When you gave in to fear, you were giving in to him. His method is fear. God's method is love. He loves you. He died for you. You belong to Him. He wants you to live in love, not fear. Perfect love casts out fear."

Amazingly, from that time on, she was totally delivered. She stayed at Hena's home for about a month and was doing well. Then she returned to Monrovia. She got into a church there. For several years afterward, I always remembered to ask about her. Hena told me she was still doing fine. She had been totally delivered from Satan's grip by God's love.

19
Occasionally Clueless

After we had moved from ELWA to Kolahun, it wasn't long before other SIM missionaries came into the area. We were scattered among various villages in the region. I was appointed area team leader, but I never felt comfortable in that role. My heart was in the villages, not checking in on staff. We were a diverse group, both in our gifting and in our nationalities. Among us there were twenty staff members from nine different countries – America, Canada, Australia, New Zealand, Germany, Korea, Taiwan, Hong Kong and Wales. It was a challenge to be constantly immersed in a second culture, and adding multiple ethnicities to the mix made our intercultural experience even more colorful.

An Asian couple came to our home the first time for dinner and afterward we were sitting around talking. It was getting pretty late, but they just kept hanging around. We had run out of steam and conversation long ago, and Jeanette and I were ready for bed. But they just kept on staying, even though they were yawning as much as we were. Jeanette and I were wondering why they didn't excuse themselves and call it an evening. As the night wore on, somehow we stumbled into a discussion about how we say good night in our respective cultures. Come to find out, in their culture the host is expected to let the guests know when it's time for them to leave. So while we were wondering why they wouldn't go, they were wondering why we hadn't been gracious enough to dismiss them.

Paul and Grace Chiang, came from Taiwan and Hong Kong. They were working in a Muslim village called Polowu, which is where I had met the man standing in the middle of the road. It was a slow go for them to get a ministry started there. It was also a lonely ministry, but I really didn't know how to help them in Muslim evangelism. Their mother-tongues were Mandarin and Cantonese, speaking only Mandarin between them. Besides that, they were trying to communicate the gospel in English. It was hard enough for them to communicate with each other, let alone with the rest of the world. When Paul came to Liberia, he wanted to get right down to business with us, despite the language barriers. The Americans among us wanted to start off getting to know them with small talk. I would joke around with Paul, but he never realized that I was joking. It got so confusing to him that he stopped responding when I asked him to do something. He was accustomed to straight-talk from a leader, not humor. So when I did start talking directly to him about what I wanted him to do, he thought I was only making suggestions.

And then there were the folks from Australia and New Zealand who wanted to be given several options to choose from. They took directives as an offense to their intelligence. But they didn't mind speaking their minds about how they honestly felt toward others.

Add to that the differences of temperaments between individuals and you had quite a party going on. Some people were talkative, others were private, and some were sensitive, while others were clueless. Some liked to joke and others couldn't take one. I felt more at ease working in the villages than I did leading my missionary colleagues.

But I loved and respected each one of them. We were each called by God to reach out to the Gbandi people and the neighboring tribes. Despite our differences, we were a family, each of us one of God's peculiar people. We had monthly gatherings for prayer and mutual encouragement. We sometimes had picnics just for fun and relaxation. Like all families, we had our own little quirks. Some of us seemed to be quirkier than others. We were once picnicking at a place along a river where the villagers had stretched a vine monkey-bridge over it. A young short-termer edged halfway across it and then let out a piercing, echoing Tarzan yell. He got quite a kick out of himself doing that, but the villagers took his call very seriously. They came running to the river to save whoever had fallen in. When it was explained to them that it was a false alarm, they couldn't understand why anyone would do such a thing. Tarzan calls did not register with them at all. It wasn't those villagers who were clueless. It was one of our very own.

I've been known to be clueless on occasion myself. I could definitely get preoccupied with my work and lose sight of what was happening in our own family. There was never an end to people needing to be reached with the gospel. That's why Jeanette made sure I didn't lose touch with our kids by working too much. She used to say "There is no replacing time with the kids." This is true. The girls grew up so fast, and they were also growing up far away from us during their school years. We needed to make the most of the time we had with them on their Christmas, Easter and summer breaks.

Having grown up in a family that never took vacations, it was a real adjustment for me to fall in with Jeanette's resolve to take weekly family outings, plus a yearly vacation. But once I got the hang of it, I started looking forward to time away with the family. I'll admit to sometimes slipping a little ministry into our getaways, but I always had fun with Jeanette and the girls. It helped me to be less serious all the time, and my girls told me it meant the world to them.

Each week we tried to find a different place to enjoy. Liberia is a great place for simple outings. The canopy of the jungle is beautiful and is ideal for hiking and picnicking. To be culturally sensitive, we stayed away from mountains and other places the people considered sacred. We also had to watch out for snakes and be careful around parasitic bodies of water, but there was always something new to explore. The girls loved a place along a creek that had natural swinging vines hanging from the trees. They would jump from the ravine cliff and swing out over the valley on a vine. Debbie once slipped off the vine and fell into the creek only to scramble back up the cliff to try it again.

A family outing at the monkey bridge

On our vacations we often drove down to the ocean beach at ELWA, where it was safe and comfortable. We had a lot of fun playing volleyball, swimming and relaxing by the ocean. This helped the girls to see another side of me.

Usually when we drove the 270 miles from Kolahun to Monrovia, it was not relaxing for anyone. I wanted to make fast time and I didn't want to stop for anything, not even for bathroom breaks. When I did stop, those bathrooms were just a bush along the side of the road. In the hot dry season the road was bumpy and dusty. If I opened the hatch on the roof of our Toyota truck, the dust would swirl inside along with the exhaust fumes and everyone would be coughing and gasping for air. If I kept it closed, it would get so hot in there they would nearly drown in their own perspiration. The girls would sing for hours to keep from getting carsick. But we knew it would be relaxing when we finally got to ELWA.

After a couple years of renting the house in Kolahun, I started thinking it was a waste of the Lord's money to continually pay a high monthly rent. I thought it would be a better investment both for us and for the ministry to buy a piece of land and build our own house. I had also grown concerned about our growing girls playing with some of the local kids. Young Liberian girls have responsibilities very early on, in caring for their younger siblings. So it was only young boys hanging around. We just needed more space and more privacy.

I tried to find a plot on the edge of town, but the closest one I could find was a mile away. It was a ten-acre plot, set out in the middle of verdant green previously farmed land. It was beautiful surroundings for a home. The idea was to build not only a house, but also an area mission headquarters and a building for housing the Discipleship Training Center.

God provided the money through SIM and many friends and supporters. Jeanette's father was especially generous. I hired a few men and we built the house using compressed mud and cement blocks. I made the door and window frames and framed all the rafters. We added a large attic for missionaries to store their belongings when they went on furlough. I made a solar electric panel for lighting and erected a sun-powered hot water system. We dug a well and installed a pump for running water. With those conveniences, we were well-off by African standards. I also built a large shed where I could do my fix-it projects. Once again, my handiness was a help to other missionaries who needed a car or a motorcycle repaired.

The soil on the property was not the best for growing a vegetable garden because it had been cut and burned over so many times. But we managed to put in a suitable garden. I planted some fruit trees and Jeanette planted many beautiful tropical flowers around the house. The soil wasn't very fertile, but with tender care we made it produce for us. It was very restful and a nice place to call home. It was especially good when the girls were home with us from school. But it was almost too quiet when they were away. When they were home during the summers and holidays, they filled the house with lots of noise and laughter and sometimes a little bickering.

I acquired an old piano and replaced the strings with some old wires. It didn't sound very good, but it was somewhat musical. Jeanette and the girls played it and we sang hymns around it as a family. Much of the time the girls sewed and baked, while also enjoying reading and playing sports outside. Around the property, the girls shot snakes and pesky birds, the ones that were apt to destroy crops. We often played games and laughed at the dinner table, but after a bit I would leave to study the Bible or work on one of my projects. I could get so consumed with all I had to do, there were times I needed a reminder from Jeanette to take a break. When I was in my shop fixing something, I was miles away from all the pressure of ministry. It was just the break I needed.

The Lord reminded me that I also needed to again take seriously my role as priest in our family, so I started praying more often for Jeanette and the girls. Jeanette was already praying for them. I also took seriously leading family devotions, but maybe sometimes a little too seriously. Because the girls were away at boarding school for so much of the year, and I was often away teaching while they were with us, I tried to make up for lost time with my family. To me, the best time to do this was just before dinner when we were already seated together. Sometimes I'd go on for a long time and dinner would get cold. The girls' complaints about the cold food did not deter me. We had a large world map on the wall beside the table, so we took additional time each meal to pray for a missionary family we knew.

Sometimes I took one of the girls along with me to a village where I would be preaching. One time Joyce was riding with me on my motorcycle when a herd of goats charged across the road. I hit one of them and the motorcycle slid sideways. I did all I could to protect Joyce from falling to the ground. She landed on top of me, which I was happy about, but my body took quite a beating.

My hand and my leg got badly skinned. But at least Joyce was all right. As a dad, that's all that mattered to me.

We also went as a family to the villages to invite people to come to church. I was always happy to have my girls helping me in the work. Usually the villagers were working in their farms and we called them to come to an evening service. We would usually get a good-sized group to come out. We sang and worshiped and I preached along with a translator.

Christmas was a big day of celebration for the believers in Liberia. We had a morning service in the village hall that lasted at least three hours. If I wasn't preaching, we'd sit among the people, not understanding the message. But even if we couldn't understand the words of the songs, we could always catch the spirit of their worship. After the service the people often butchered a goat; then everyone enjoyed spicy goat soup on rice.

It was usually too late for us to celebrate when we finally returned home, so we had our own celebration the next morning. The girls gave out handmade gifts that they had placed beneath our homely old aluminum Christmas tree. We kept the tree hidden in the back bedroom lest the nationals should think we had fallen into idolatry, worshiping a tree like the pagans did. We also read the Christmas story from the Bible and ate a meal of spam and potatoes, or sometimes a tough chicken from the market, topped off with freshly baked cinnamon rolls.

On two occasions a lady in America, whom the girls called the "silly goose lady," because she owned a thrift store called The Silly Goose, sent us a huge box filled with used clothing and other items from her store. Jeanette determined which things would be best for each daughter. They were thrilled to find all sorts of things to wear, including lots of practical items. Joyce treasured an old alarm clock she got. The girls got a box of partially used makeup and Reenie received a 70's-style dress with puffy shoulders. Shari's jewelry box was a treasure for many years. They didn't care if the gifts were used and out-of-date. In fact it made every Christmas after that seem wonderful because somebody had thought of us.

None of us can remember how or when we first met William Mahe, but we all fondly remember him as a part of our family. We didn't know how old he was, nor did he. William was one of those ageless people. He was kind of slow and a little mentally unbalanced, so maybe he had just forgotten his age. But it didn't matter. He lived in a village about seven miles from us, and he hobbled the distance every day just to sweep our house. He had an ugly ulcer on his leg which never improved, so he shuffled along, just shoving the dirt around. He couldn't sweep very much in a day – maybe half a room. But in his mind he was working. Even when he wasn't feeling well, he would walk all the way just to tell us he couldn't work that day. We offered to pay him, but he didn't want much. He only wanted enough to sustain himself each day, maybe a little rice or money to buy dried fish. He was concerned he might get robbed if he had much money.

Sometimes he needed new flip-flops or a new bucket to catch rain off the roof, so we gave him that for payment. One time we found a big dead bush rat under our clothesline and he was so excited to take it home and share it with people in his village. We also gave him money to buy penicillin powder for his ulcer. But mostly he just enjoyed being with us, as we enjoyed him.

William had a simple but obvious love for the Lord. He often told us that he prayed

William Mahe,
beloved friend of the family

for our family every day. He said he was so glad we had come to Liberia to tell the people about Jesus. Sometimes he would have an off-day and he would start talking to the trees, but even then he had a happy shine on his face. His love for the Lord radiated from his heart.

It wasn't necessary to always be having your best day to fit in with our family. It was okay with us if you talked to the trees once in a while, or even if you were occasionally kind of clueless.

20
Finding the Key

The gospel took root in Gbandi hearts like the seed we planted in our infertile garden. Something seemed to be hindering them from growing deeply in the truth of God. Years later, after the country had gone through the upheaval of civil war, and the believers there had endured horrible suffering, I finally understood the holdup. But I couldn't put my finger on it while I

Jeanette holding a child as she often did in the villages

still had my hands to the plow.

The Lord used me to plant a small church in Kolahun and some other gatherings in surrounding villages. It was always hard tilling. The groups usually amounted to half a dozen to maybe twenty people. We called these gatherings "outreach points," not churches, because they were not fully functional. This was mainly because there were no biblically qualified leaders among them. We tried to address this in the Discipleship Training Center. It was a three-year Bible-teaching program for developing leadership in the newly started outreach points. The teaching was pretty basic because most of the men we worked with were new believers. We appointed leaders of the outreach gatherings, but we were careful not to call them pastors or elders or even deacons. I now think it was a mistake for us to even call them leaders, but in our eagerness to get something going, we did it anyway. Hindsight always makes you wiser than you were when you were groping through your mistakes.

I mentioned earlier that some missionaries say there is a "key" for unlocking every cultural door to the gospel. Whether or not this is true, I was convinced that the Word is the master key for every culture. But I also kept looking for a "key man" whom the Lord was raising up for me to disciple. I was looking and praying for a man who was really thirsting to live for the Lord. In Ethiopia, God had given me some men like that and I was expecting to find the same in Liberia. The first place I looked was in our Discipleship Training Center. But I felt I was hearing more lip-service from the students there than honest answers.

Hena was a key man, but I couldn't train him as much as I would have liked because of our language barrier and his lack of education. His illiteracy gave him a diminished standing in the eyes of the younger people, though he came to be respected by everyone years later. I greatly appreciated him as a friend and I admired his faith.

The Lord's recipe for making a man after His own heart was different from my way. I had no idea it would take a civil war for Him to refine the other leaders He had chosen for His church in

Liberia. Having gone through all that before in Ethiopia, I was hoping it would be easier this time. But it wasn't. It was worse.

I had once assumed that, when I got to be an older, seasoned missionary, the work would also get easier. It didn't. It got harder. After all, Jesus promised trouble to anyone who was willing to follow and serve Him. So the farther I went with Him, the more trouble I got. But it did get easier for me to cast my cares on Him, because holding onto them just increased my burden. I spent many a night praying my heart out and shedding tears because of the burden I felt for the people. I rose early in the mornings to read the Word and seek the Lord's presence and power.

The false churches in the area had tried to buy the people's allegiance, which wound up creating a "gimme" mindset among them toward the missionaries. Jesus had the same problem during His life and ministry. He was popular with the masses as long as He was doing miracles and feeding them. But when He came to the crux of His life mission, everyone deserted Him.

I tried to be friendly to everyone I met, gladly taxiing people in my truck here and there, if I was going their way and sometimes even when I wasn't. The believers were few and they were scattered among various villages, so we decided to arrange Bible teaching conferences so that they could congregate and learn together. The church in Kolahun wasn't too far from any of the villages, and they were used to walking that distance. But then, when it came time for the conference, everyone started demanding a ride. Two or three other missionaries were involved with the conference and they each had cars. They were also willing to drive people. But it got out-of-hand. If we drove some, we had to drive them all. As the gatherings got larger, it became a fiasco. If we didn't offer them a ride, they wouldn't come to the conference. It became a vicious cycle.

This also went on in the Discipleship Training Center. There was a young guy, maybe 20 years old, who started to agitate the other students. He started telling the others, "These missionaries are getting lots of money from their countries and it is supposed to be for us. They are just helping themselves to our money. They live in large houses and they ride motorcycles and drive cars. Then they send us out on foot to do the outreach. They should be supplying us with motorcycles. And look at the Training Center building. It is not a good building like their homes. They are taking all these things for themselves."

The grievances kept piling up against us. Guys were getting annoyed because they couldn't get a ride on demand to wherever they might be heading. There was a growing sense of animosity among them and so it was impossible to teach them. Finally I had a meeting with some of the main instigators. I wanted to bring everything out in the open for discussion. I was willing to listen to all of their complaints. The young agitator said, "John, we want to first meet in private, so please step outside."

When I came back inside the young man said, "John, we are thankful to you for bringing the gospel to us, but from now on we are going to take the leadership. When we want you to participate with us, we will call on you."

I thought I had good relationships with some of the guys, so I asked them, "Is this what you all have agreed upon?"

They all agreed that it was what they wanted. I felt like I was being pushed out. We ended the meeting and I went home feeling pretty low. I knew that if I gave any pushback, our work there would be done. They would just join with some other group.

During that week I went to every village and spoke personally with each leader and asked if I could hear their grievances against me and the SIM mission. One guy confessed to me that he didn't really agree with the group decision. When I asked him why he had gone along with it, he said he was thinking something good for him could come out of it. He meant that he was hoping we would cave into their threats and give him some money to stay with us. It was all for personal gain, the very thing they had accused us of doing.

I set up another meeting with the village outreach leaders. An African-American pastor named Alfred Williams was with me. I read from the Scriptures the biblical qualifications for leadership. I reminded them that up to that point we had not recognized anyone among them as pastors, elders or deacons because they were still young believers and we did not feel they were yet qualified to serve in those capacities. I asked them, "According to these biblical standards, do any of you believe you are qualified to lead?'

I could see that they were feeling humbled by God's Word. No one said a word. Pastor Williams then spoke up and, looking at each guy, he said, "What about you? Are you qualified to lead?"

He went around the room asking every guy the same question. They all told him they were not qualified to lead, including the young guy who had instigated the whole uprising. God used that meeting to help the men make their own self-judgments. It didn't clear up everything, but it helped them to see the condition of their own hearts more clearly than before. When that started to happen, they began to be more teachable. The Lord was still just scratching the surface, but He was also softening the soil of their hearts.

For some time there were rumors that one of the leaders of the church in Kolahun had taken a second wife in another village. It was also said that he had fathered a child with her. I called on him and asked if the rumor was true. He assured me it was not. But then another brother, who came from a different tribe, came up with two witnesses who stated that this first man did have a second wife. I called for another meeting to get to the bottom of it. I didn't know the man was present in the meeting. I publicly pressed the pastor to find out if he would vouch for the man's denial. He was hesitant to speak, but he realized the implications of lying about a matter like this. Reluctantly he said, "I have to admit, he has two wives."

It was not until years later, after the civil war, when I met again with some of the men who were in that meeting, that I learned how offensive that day of disclosure had been to them. One of their own had betrayed a fellow tribesman to the white man. The man had been exposed and shamed. I was the bad guy for exposing the sin that had been denied. Even though each of them had known the truth of the matter, they had turned a blind eye to it. But this was not nearly as wrong as it was to be disloyal to another Gbandi. To them, this was the unpardonable sin.

This was not merely a black versus white problem. It was also an inter-tribal matter. The man who had informed me about the brother with two wives was from another tribe, and they trusted him no more than me. In Africa, most of the wars are not political or between nations. They are tribal wars. Tribal allegiance is far more important than national loyalty. The civil war in Liberia scrambled the whole country, including all the tribes. People fled for their lives to refugee camps in neighboring countries and were forced to live mixed in with all the other tribes. By the time I had located some of those Gbandi church leaders in camps in Sierra Leone and Guinea, tribal differences didn't matter to them anymore. They were glad to see me again, and I was glad to see them, still alive. The war had taken an awful human toll, but God had used it to accomplish more than I or any believer could do. He used the war to cause the people to seek Him with hungry hearts.

I learned another secret when I found some of the young men in the camps who had gone through our Training Center. All along, each of them had been drinking palm wine and getting intoxicated. Sometimes they drank and partied together. But they all knew what the others were doing. They had just been keeping it a secret from the white man. Sin blocked their growth and maturity.

And so I finally came to understand what had been holding back most of the Gbandi leaders from living fully for the Lord. But the key to helping them was not my knowing their sins. The key was to love them and to help them grow in the knowledge of God's love for them in Christ. The key was in my heart all along, even when my hands were still at the plow.

21
Is There a Way Back?

In 1989 we were on furlough in Seattle when civil war erupted in Liberia. It came suddenly and swiftly. Samuel Doe had kept a firm hand on the country, warding off a few previous coups. He just tightened his grip when that happened. He banned political opposition parties, he shut down newspapers and he rigged a fraudulent election. He killed many of his political opponents and appointed people from his own Krahn tribe to key government positions. With all its political corruption, Liberia was crumbling economically. There was always an unhappy stir in the air among the people. It was nothing we worried about. It was just the air we breathed there.

Then an American-born Liberian named Charles Taylor charged into the country from Ivory Coast with packs of highly armed rebels he had recruited from Sierra Leone. He was backed by the ruthless Libyan dictator, Muammar Gaddafi. Taylor was also a brutal killer. He pitted tribe against tribe and, taking advantage of the chaos he created, he stormed through the country toward Monrovia, killing and pillaging along a path of terror. A West African coalition force teamed with the government to push back his rebels from the capital before an uneasy truce was called.

We stayed an additional year in Seattle, waiting for things to settle down. When the coast was clear, I returned in July of 1991 to Liberia, with Jeanette and Joyce following a month later. It was Joyce's final year of high school and she chose to go back to Africa with us. After going through a war in Ethiopia, I knew it would be important to keep in good contact with folks at home, especially now that our four oldest daughters would be left behind in college or in raising their own families. They feared for our safety, so I took up learning Morse code and got my ham radio operator's license. Friends from Dever Conner Community Church gave us a ham radio. The first thing to do before going out to the mission field is to gather prayer support and set up a good line of communication. I arranged with a ham operator in Chicago to link my radio transmissions to the girls by phone.

After landing in Monrovia aboard a U.N. flight from Sierra Leone, I went first to the ELWA compound. I was blown away by the sight of all the destruction there. The rebels had burned down the studio building, the powerhouse and the transmitter building. The print shop was burned along with six or eight houses. Every other building on the site had been shot up. Over 2,000 magnificent palm trees that had once towered over the grounds,

Our first home, war damaged and destroyed

had been chopped down. I knew what it meant – the people had been starving and they had cut down those trees to get the coconuts and the cabbage tops. In their desperation, they had sacrificed those beautiful trees for their own survival. As I later saw, palm trees had been toppled all over the country. Food was desperately scarce. This was heart wrenching.

I walked about in a daze. The hospital was still standing and the pharmacy was still there, although both buildings had been totally looted. All of the furniture and equipment were gone as well as the doors and windows. I walked to the International Church of Monrovia building. This is where we had attended church as a family when we were at ELWA. It had a huge mortar hole in one side. I walked through the hole. Inside, I looked at a wall with a big wooden map of Africa with a cross and the words "Jesus Christ Is Lord" inscribed on it. I just stood there whispering, "Why, Lord?" The gospel had been going out all over Africa through ELWA broadcasts, and now the radio station was completely destroyed. But as I stood there looking over the ruins, those words struck my heart: "Jesus Christ is Lord." I couldn't help

A very poignant reminder in difficult times

falling to my knees, worshiping Him, and thanking Him that His plans and purposes never change. Even though everything had fallen apart, He was still Lord of all.

I wandered around the compound for a couple more hours. Occasionally I found a human bone or a skull. It was an eerie scene. I felt an awful grief as I pondered how much the people had suffered.

To prepare the way for Jeanette to come back to Liberia, I found a house at ELWA near a large lagoon by the ocean. It had formerly been a lovely place, but now it looked ransacked and broken. But it was livable. I counted 56 bullet marks on its walls. It too had been totally looted.

In the streets you could buy just about anything – all stuff that had been pillaged from other places. I bought doors and window frames and some passable furniture. I patched holes in the walls and gave the house a rough inside paint job just to make it look presentable. Jeanette would add her feminine touch after she came to our new home.

At first, movement in the countryside was restricted due to the instability and skirmishes still going on. When it calmed, people who purchased official documentation were permitted to travel in regulated areas. But that didn't happen until 1992. Meanwhile, I started reaching out to the soldiers from the coalition forces who were supporting the Liberian government. I met with them in various military camps, sharing the gospel and leading Bible studies. I was privileged to help several young men from Ghana, Nigeria, Senegal and other countries find the Lord. I had them filling out Bible study workbooks and then Jeanette corrected them. She also started visiting children in an orphanage. Orphans were everywhere, many living on the streets, begging.

During the impasse, the government offered amnesty to young rebels who wanted to return to their homes, on condition that they lay down their arms and undergo a rehabilitation program. I offered to lead the men in Bible studies twice a week. It was set up as an informal Bible school and it included about 20 young men from both sides of the battle. Many of them had been forced into service by the rebels. All of them had deep psychological wounds and great burdens of guilt for the things they had done. Some years later I met a man who had attended that school. He had become a church pastor. He told me he knew of three other former rebels who had participated in the Bible school and who had also become pastors. It is always amazing to me how the Lord can turn such turmoil into something good. He changed the angry hearts of those rebels and gave them hearts to love and serve His people. The inscription inside that ruined church building said it all: "Jesus Christ Is Lord."

I wanted to check on the Gbandi churches, so I made four trips north in 1992. On one of those trips, Jeanette went with me, along with African-American Pastor Williams, his wife, a friend named Jackie Exum, and Liberian Pastor Sayndee.

The road from Monrovia to Kolahun was guarded by coalition troops for the first ten miles outside the city. The next 270 miles up-country were tightly controlled by Taylor's rebel forces. There were 32 checkpoints along the way. At the check points they all wanted money. I never gave them any. Instead, I gave them gospel tracts or Bibles. They took the Bibles, figuring they could sell them.

At one checkpoint I drove up to the gate and was halted by a rebel who was obviously drunk. With slurred speech he demanded I tell him what I was doing there. After questioning me for a while, he finally let me pass through, but he ordered me to pull over just past the gate. Three commanders came ambling out of a building and they all started peppering me at once with questions and commands. They were yelling and hollering at me as though they were competing against each other over who had the most power. One wanted to see our documents. Another demanded to look through our bags. The third one ordered us to go into the building.

Jeanette and the others went inside the building while I remained outside with the vehicle. I knew they could take it from us if they wanted to do so. After a few minutes Jeanette called me to come inside the building. When I walked inside, one of the commanders was telling another to let us pass. But the second commander pulled a hand grenade from his belt and shouted, "If anyone makes another move, I'll blow us all up!"

His name was Commando Benjamin. He was a middle-aged man wearing dark sunglasses, which he occasionally lifted from his face. When he looked at us without his glasses covering his eyes, he spoke to us in a friendly manner. But when he slid his glasses back over his eyes, he started ranting and threatening us. This went on for about two hours. Meanwhile, he kept playing with that grenade like it was a little ball in his hand. We didn't know what he was ranting about or what he was going to do to us. But it seemed he was just trying to show us how powerful he was. Amazingly, I felt no fear. Maybe he could sense it, because he suddenly announced, "You can go," as if he had tired of playing with us.

When we walked outside, I noticed that a tire was flat on our vehicle. I pulled out a tire wrench and a jack to lift it up, but Commando Benjamin shouted, "You can't do that here! This is a checkpoint. You must drive on!"

I just ignored him and started jacking up the vehicle. Pastor Williams walked over to him and started exhorting him, "This is not how to work with people." He explained how he could improve his way of leading others. Commando Benjamin just stood there listening to him. I couldn't change that tire fast enough and barely tightened the lug nuts. I didn't know when he might put on his dark glasses again and pull out that hand grenade.

We piled into the vehicle and took off. Down the way, I pulled over and tightened the nuts. We were all glad to get away from the commando with the dark sunglasses.

When we arrived at our house in Kolahun, Jeanette and I were not surprised to see that it had been looted. We had heard that a rebel commander had liked it and so he had used it as his quarters for a while. Before he left, he loaded up everything he could fit on a truck. The windows and doors were gone along with the electrical wiring and other hardware. The solar panels for lighting and hot water were missing. He took everything that was even remotely worthwhile.

Even the steps to the attic were gone. Jeanette and I scaled up the risers and sorted through scraps scattered on the floor. Jeanette found a few little Scripture promise cards that we had recited during meals with our children. One of the cards read, *"Be still and know that I am God."*[16] I put it inside my wallet and I have carried it with me ever since that day. The rebels didn't want that, but to us it was the most precious thing they could have left. Jeanette remarked that they had taken everything from us but the thing they needed the most.

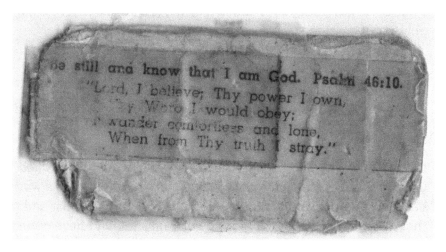

Carried in my wallet for almost 20 years

The people in the churches were excited to see us. Each person had horrible stories to tell. Many people had fled the area. Young men and boys had been conscripted into service. Many had been killed or were still hiding in the forests. They had needed to forage for food. But when the people heard that we had returned, they came out, dancing in the streets. We held a conference in Fassavolo. What a joyous reunion! We could not stay long, but we did all we could to encourage the people.

Taylor's forces were holed up in an area called Gbarnga, which is located just beyond the turn-off to Kolahun. We had passed a few checkpoints along that dirt road when we came to another, where a rebel told us we could not go further without special permission granted from Taylor's headquarters. He ordered us to turn around and go back to Gbarnga. Gas cost upward of $10 a gallon and it was hard to come by. It could only be purchased in cans from people who were selling it along the road. It was diluted to the point that the vehicle's engine constantly pinged and sometimes barely ran. I didn't want to waste gas backtracking twenty miles, but I had no choice. The man insisted, saying that he would accompany us there.

About a half mile from Gbarnga, the rebel told me to stop the vehicle. He got out and just walked away. It was all a ruse. He had only wanted a ride.

I decided to go on to their headquarters, figuring if I got more papers I wouldn't have that problem again. As I pulled up to the gate, a young teenage boy holding an AK-47 stopped me. He waved me through and I went on to the main office. When I filled out the paper, I wrote down that I was from ELWA. They were all familiar with ELWA. Many believers had been pulled into the war out of a sense of duty to their tribes. One guy in the office edged up to me and asked with tears welling in his eyes, "Is there a way back to God?" He opened up to me, saying he was a Baptist and that he had done some things in the war he shouldn't have done. He was deeply troubled and weighed down with guilt. He kept pleading in tears, "Is there a way back?" I was able to share some Scriptures promising God's forgiveness in Jesus Christ. I led him in a prayer of restoration to the Lord.

Once again, I could see the truth of that inscription on the church wall: "Jesus Christ is Lord!" He had used the ruse of one man to lead me to the need of another. It was worth going all those extra miles to help that man find his way back to God.

By August of 1992, the situation in the country was getting tense again. We were beginning to think about our exit strategy. I figured each road trip would probably be my last. Heading back to ELWA on what would be our final trip, we were stopped at a checkpoint by a guard holding an AK-47. He said we could not go any farther because it was now past curfew. Pointing his weapon at me, he ordered me out of the vehicle. He said they needed it to transport a wounded soldier. I knew that this was another ruse. He was trying to steal my truck. I told him, "No." He grabbed his weapon tightly, pointing its barrel at my feet.

"Are you resisting my authority?" he demanded.

I just stood there saying nothing. Soldiers started gathering all around us. He kept asking if I was disobeying him. I stood my ground, saying nothing. He stood glaring at me with a confused expression on his face. He didn't know what to do with me. He had probably shot people for no reason at all, but he didn't know how to handle someone who was defying him.

Just then, a Toyota pickup pulled up. The driver got out and asked, "Who is driving this truck?" When he found out it was me, he said, "Okay, you can pass."

I turned to the angry rebel and said, "I'm sorry, but I have to go now. Good bye." He was still clutching his rifle when I drove away.

In just a few hundred more yards there was another checkpoint. Again I was ordered to pull over and park the vehicle due to the curfew. I was told to go inside a building. The Toyota pickup again pulled up behind us and the driver came inside, followed by a 4-star general from the rebel army. He introduced himself as General Musa. He told me he had been educated in America and that he was the highest ranking field commander in Taylor's forces. I knew he was a murderous guy, but he seemed to want to be friendly with me. He told me I was free to go.

But I paused and asked him, "May I say something?" He said, "Sure."

I told him I was from ELWA. He said he was aware of that, and he knew what we did at ELWA. Pastor Sayndee was with me. He asked the general if we could pray for him. He said he would love to be prayed for. So Pastor Sayndee prayed a very heartfelt prayer for the general and his forces and for the entire country of Liberia. He was deeply moved. He smiled and said, "Thank you very much!"

The high-commander then ordered another commander to take us through all the remaining gates that were under rebel control. Jesus stated that He would build His church and the gates of hell would not prevail against it. Because He is Lord of all, He even used the keepers of hell's gates to open them up for His glory.

22
Shredded By War

A young man from Northern Liberia somehow made his way through the dangerous countryside to our home near Monrovia. Jerry had left his wife and small child upcountry and, having heard of the Coreys, he thought we could perhaps help rescue them. It took him two weeks to find his way through miles of jungle and armed rebels, and by the time he came to us, he was nearly scared out of his mind. The killing rampages in the country were brutal beyond comprehension, and he had seen too much. Along the roads, human skulls were propped on the tops of poles. Children were murdered or maimed in front of their parents or kidnapped and forced to fight for the rebels. Jerry moved only by night, even while patrols constantly prowled the forest searching for "spies."

Jerry stayed with us for two weeks. He couldn't sleep and he kept having flashbacks of the horrors he had seen along his flight, sometimes hallucinating and crying out, "There they are! They are coming to kill us!" He was replaying in his mind those close encounters he had with the rebels who had chased down and killed innocent people before his eyes. With the fighting flaring up again, there was nothing we could do to help him retrieve his family. We could only help him regain his mind and heart.

In losing his mind, Jerry had lost his bearing. He didn't know where he was or who he was. All I knew to help him was to read Scriptures to him, particularly passages that declared who he was in Christ. Jerry wanted to listen to cassette tapes of worshipful music sung by The Brooklyn Tabernacle Choir. He wanted it played loudly day and night. This calmed his mind and slowly helped him to get grounded in reality. It didn't bring his family to him, but it brought him the peace of Christ that is even more incomprehensible than the terror of war.

But it was still a horrifying reality for him to face. War wears on the soul. Constantly living on red alert drains the mind dry. I couldn't imagine what Jerry was going through, being separated from his wife and child with no way to reach them. We, at least, had a ham radio to keep in touch with our girls.

Communicating with our girls through ham radio

In July of 1992, Joyce graduated from high school and left for college in Canada. That got her out of harm's way, which made us feel relieved. We kept in contact with the girls as often as we could. Living near the ocean, we had much better radio waves than we would have had if we were living inland. I was able to repair a 70-foot tower at the ELWA site for broadcasting. It was a little cumbersome to communicate with them saying "over" after each statement, but that was nothing compared to the sound of distant gunshots the girls could hear in the background over the radio. They had heard those sounds before in Ethiopia, and it frightened them to think that we were in the middle of that again.

Charles Taylor made another strong offensive toward the capital in October of 1992. The rebels were swarming just over a hill from us – maybe a mile away – when we were talking with Reenie and her husband, Darren. Suddenly Reenie heard the airwaves erupting with popping noises in the background. All she could hear me saying was, "Oh, that's gunfire. I've got to go!" The radio went dead and none of the girls heard from us again for another two weeks.

Not knowing what had happened to us during that time, the girls worried so much they could barely eat or breathe. Joyce slept in the dorm hallway by the phone booth for two weeks. It was also a tremendous stress on Jeanette and me to have no contact with them. I could see how Jerry had lost his mind for worry. It weighed heavily on Jeanette to know the girls would be so frantic. But they prayed hard for us. In her typically direct manner, Reenie prayed, "Oh, God, what use is Dad to you dead, and to die in this way? Don't you have anything further for him to do on this earth? What glory do you receive through this madness?"

God's answers to direct prayers don't always come immediately, but they do come.

Jeanette and I were already packed and ready to go at a moment's notice, but we were still holding out to see what God would do in all the chaos. All we had was one small handbag apiece weighing fifteen pounds. The Monrovia airport, far outside the city, was cut off to us, but there was a small grass airstrip inside the city where small planes could land and take off. I had a very bad back injury. It was excruciating for me to even move, let alone move quickly. So if we had to move out suddenly, I wasn't sure I would make the plane. All I could manage was to lie down and listen to rockets launched from rebel territory flying overhead and exploding somewhere in or near Monrovia.

A curfew in our area was set for six o'clock in the evening. It was very dangerous to be outside after that hour. A person lurking in the dark could be shot on sight. Knowing we had to evacuate the next day, we headed toward a Lutheran mission station closer to the airstrip.

During the night the fighting subsided because the rebels had swung around to the other side of town to launch a surprise attack. It was calm again near ELWA. We hadn't told any of the nationals that we were planning to leave, so we made our way around to as many of them as we could find. We invited them to come to our house and we gave away all of our possessions – clothes, furniture, everything, whatever they could carry. We had been through all of this before, and judging by the degree of terror ripping apart the country, we sensed that we would not be able to come back soon.

Saying goodbye to people who were in such distress was almost too much for us to bear. It broke Jeanette's heart to leave the young Liberians who'd become like part of our family. Her heart is driven by love and mercy. Mine is driven by the message and the mission. It went against every fiber of our being to say goodbye again to the people God had called us to serve. In the Lord, they were all like children to us. Jeanette felt such grief, she could hardly say goodbye. We could leave, but they were cornered on one side by the ocean and on the other side by the rebel forces.

The next day we made it to the airstrip in the middle of the day. A small airplane was still transporting people out of the country to Ivory Coast. It was the only way left to get out of Liberia. The main airport had been overrun during the night by the rebels. The plane we boarded was very small. Another missionary couple was flying out with us. As we taxied to the end of the grass runway that ended close to a swamp, the man remarked to me, "You know, rebels could come out of there and attack us before we could even take off."

We were in the air about 45 minutes when the pilot informed us that the airstrip had just been closed. It had been overrun by rebels who had come through the swamp. God's answers to direct prayers don't always come immediately, but they do come, in God's perfect time.

It had been two frightful weeks since we had lost communication with the girls. With few words and lots of tears, each received a phone call from us, saying we were safe in Ivory Coast and were coming back to the United States. We still couldn't say we were coming "home" to America, because Africa was still our home. But we could say we were coming back to be with our family, because all of our girls were there by then. It would be the first time in several years that we would be together in one place.

It was terrific to be reunited with our girls. Normally we would have connected in Seattle, where we had our roots, but the Lord transplanted each of us instead to Portland. We all wound up living there for different reasons. One good reason I could see, for Jeanette and me to live in Portland, was that one of our main supporting churches, Southwest Bible Church, was based near there. Multnomah Bible College, where Shari went, was also in Portland.

At first, it was good just to have some time to recover from the trauma of war and separation. No one knew how long the war would continue in Liberia, but I was willing and ready to return as soon as possible. In the meantime, I took a role at Multnomah representing SIM, trying to inform and recruit students for missions. It didn't take me long to realize that I was once again a square peg trying to fit into a round hole. I wasn't a recruiter; I was a doer. I was feeling completely unsettled all over again. Once again, I started pacing and roaring like a caged lion.

I was driven by mission. Jeanette was driven by mercy. We were like two vehicles traveling down a highway, one in the fast lane and the other in the slow lane. We were headed in the same direction but at different speeds. I wanted Jeanette to move at my pace. But she couldn't. Mercy always moves slower than mission, not because it is any weaker, but because it carries the delicate part of the burden. We both struggled with the guilt of leaving the people we had loved back in Liberia. My answer was to go back. God's answer was to go forward.

I remembered the young rebel who had tearfully asked me, "Is there any way back to God?" He was wrestling with angst of another kind. Moved by my own grief for the people, I was asking God, "Is there any way back to Africa?"

Jeanette was struggling more deeply than I sometimes cared to hear. For two years I was pushing her to go back overseas. But one day when I was talking again about returning to Liberia, she looked me straight in the eye and said, "John, I can't take the tension of war. I can't take the separation. I can't take the conflict. I can't handle it anymore."

As I looked into her eyes, I could see how weary she had gotten from living in war. I realized that God was speaking to me. I needed to slow down and listen to my wife. Mercy doesn't speak loudly, but it does speak to those who have ears to hear. That Scripture verse in my wallet said, *"Be still and know that I am God: I will be exalted among the heathen, I will be exalted in the earth."*[17]

To me, being still felt like an unnatural activity. But I had kept that verse in my wallet for a reason. I realized that I needed to simply trust that He was still God; I needed to be still and remember that. He is still the Lord of the harvest and He is still driving the mission. He drives it as much by mercy as He does by might.

So I thanked her and said, "That settles it. We are not going back to Liberia." At that point, I did not know where the Lord was directing me, but I knew that the only way to walk with Him was to take one step at a time.

23
Transplanted

I struggled as a missionary recruiter. I told students at Multnomah a lot of exciting stories about how God was reaching people in other parts of the world. But I wasn't great at personally engaging with them. Most of them liked a guy who would just hang out with them and get to know them on a personal level. I was too serious for doing much of that. After speaking to so many students, I started losing track of who I had spoken to, and so I kept getting their names mixed up. I'm pretty sure that didn't make a very favorable impression on them. I stuck with it for about a year and a half, but to my knowledge not even one student went into foreign missions through my influence. I felt like a complete failure. It simply wasn't my thing.

Thankfully we were part of a healthy local church, Southwest Bible Church in Beaverton. Pastor Scott Gilchrist is one of the best Bible teachers I have ever heard. He teaches from the Scriptures verse-by-verse. The whole church is centered on Christ and the Word. The Sunday school program is solid on all levels – adult, youth and children – and there are lots of gifted teachers. There are numerous home groups that help people form good friendships and spiritual bonds and there are a growing number of people who regularly share the gospel in the community. The church is spiritually alive and warm.

At first, my only complaint was that there didn't seem to be enough of an emphasis on missions. With all the good things going on there, I could see that Southwest Bible had potential to greatly impact the world for Christ. But I was unfairly comparing the mission outreach there to the immense mission program at the church in Knoxville. While I was focusing on what was missing, I was overlooking what was actually going on there. I failed to see that there were many able teachers and boots-on-the-ground disciple-makers at Southwest, which was exactly the kind of people I had been asking the Lord to raise up to send into the harvest field. While I was grousing over my failure as a missionary recruiter at Multnomah, I also failed to see the opportunity the Lord had given me at Southwest Bible.

After the Soviet Union collapsed in late 1991, the Russian people were wide open to hearing the gospel. Duane Gilchrist, Scott's father, was working with Campus Crusade's *Jesus* film ministry, which was showing the film in schools across Russia. *Jesus* is based on the Gospel of Luke. Duane reported some amazing responses to the gospel among students, teachers and staff in the schools. Being an old by-the-book Bible teacher, I'll admit to being skeptical of those reports. I couldn't see how the gospel could be accurately presented in a film. But Duane challenged me to come with him on a trip to Eastern Russia and see for myself what God was doing there.

Along with a team from Southwest Bible and another team from a church near San Francisco, we went in the spring of 1993 to a city in East Russia called Khabarovsk. Just as Duane had reported, people there were wide open to the gospel and they were responding to *Jesus*.

By the time I arrived in Russia, the big wave of evangelism had lost some of its surge. There were scattered gatherings of new believers cropping up, mixed with a remnant of old believers who had met underground during the communist era. Most of the new converts in the schools were women and young boys and girls. The church had been so badly beaten down during the seventy years of communism, there were very few biblically trained pastors to help the people grow in their faith. The few older believers who had surfaced were usually legalistic and they had little understanding of grace.

One gathering of about ten women that I met with had the idea that a Christian's main duty to God is to keep confessing sins until the day they died. To them, the Christian life was one long confessional in which they kept punishing themselves for their sins to prove how sorry they were. If they neglected to keep current on their confessions, they were in jeopardy of missing out on heaven. They had no understanding that Christ had died to pay for their sins. The songs they sang sounded like a dirge – slow and somber. There was no joy in their voices.

I explained the gospel to them using a presentation called the line diagram, which clearly explains God's plan of salvation in Jesus Christ. Confused by false teaching, they raised a lot of objections to the gospel. Sasha, one of the female teachers who had recently trusted Christ through the *Jesus* film showing at her school, told me, "I can't understand why they can't see it. The gospel is so plain. It is so clear what Christ did for us on the cross. He has forgiven us. What more can we add to what He has done for us?"

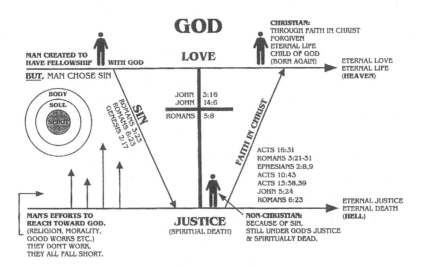

Line Diagram

There were many other misconceptions people had about the gospel. There was also a glaring lack of men in the churches. Virtually all Russian men had served in the military, and they had been taught that religion is a myth that was only fit for gullible old women and weak men. It was viewed as unmanly to believe in God, much less the gospel. Even after the government had crumbled, many men still considered it an insult to suggest there is a Creator/God.

It took me awhile to understand the way that communism had confused the souls of the Russian people, particularly the men. Russians are exceptionally intelligent and well-educated people, but communism stole their incentive. Everything and everyone belonged to the state. This reality robbed them of something that is fundamental to human nature – the drive to prosper. It especially killed the hearts of men. Drunkenness was epidemic. Many men were aimless and lethargic. They neglected their families. For generations, children had grown up without a father figure in their lives. As a result, women took over the responsibilities of raising a family, and they grew dominant out of necessity.

After I returned home from Russia, I was still hoping to get back to Africa. I could not see how a missionary to Africa could fit in Russia. But I was also struck by the obvious need to help those new Russian believers grow in the knowledge of the truth.

Jeanette continued to do spiritual battle in prayer. She has a tremendous ability to pray throughout the day while doing all kinds of tasks. She's always said it doesn't take a lot of thought to wash dishes, sweep the floor or to wipe a table. So she prays while she is working and while she is resting. She prayed that God would guide me in the way He wanted me to go.

In Ethiopia and in Liberia, I had asked God to give me key men in whom I could invest my life. He gave me Werku in Ethiopia and Hena in Liberia. I asked Him to give me His men in Russia if that was where He wanted me to serve Him.

I also asked Scott Gilchrist what he thought about me returning there. He was excited about how God was moving in

Russia and he encouraged me to go back. It occurred to me that I would probably be better at recruiting people to go with me on a mission trip than I was at persuading students to sign up for the mission field. Scott gave me his blessing to find someone from the church to accompany me to Russia. I didn't find anyone from Southwest Bible to go with me on the coming trip, but I didn't let that thought die. It was a seed that would grow into a mission project that would exceed my wildest dreams. In my thirty trips to Russia since then, quite a few church members from Southwest came with me and each was greatly used of God, reaching people in ways I could not.

An African American man, from the church I had attended as a young man in Port Angeles, went with me on my next trip to Russia. Harvey was a trained biblical counselor. He heard me speaking about my time in Russia during a prayer meeting. He later contacted me and said the Lord had impressed upon him that he ought to go. I was glad to have someone with his gifting to go along with me. The need for biblical counseling was obviously great in Russia. Harvey was also a fabulous singer. The Russians had never heard such joyful singing. Even though they couldn't

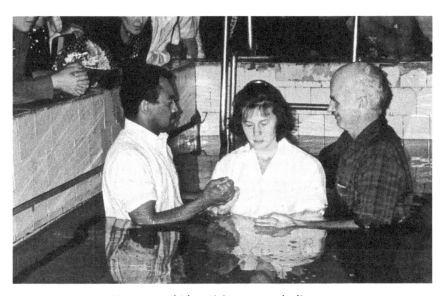

Harvey and I baptizing young believers

understand the words of the songs he sang in English, they could feel his joy and they were very uplifted.

We went back to Khabarovsk where I met with Misha, a man who had arranged our contacts with believers during our previous trip. He had a friend named Roman who was studying English. We had been invited by some teachers to go to the city of Spassk and teach a course on how to understand the Bible. The Bible was now being used in the schools for the study of history and literature. Roman wasn't a believer, but he spoke English on a basic level. I needed a translator so I asked him to help me. It happened that Roman was taking a vacation during that time, so he was free to help.

It was easy to see that Roman was not just trying to earn a few extra rubles. He was serious about improving his English. He was taking mental notes of words I had used while he was translating for me. He also kept asking me about the biblical concepts I was teaching. I could see that God was working in his heart. After about the fourth day I sat with him and, using the line diagram, I shared the gospel with him. Without any hesitation, he welcomed Christ into his heart. He was beaming with joy. I spent as much time with him as I could, building him up in his new faith. When we were leaving Spassk, he begged me to return and spend more time with him.

I returned again to Russia in February of 1995. Roman quit his job, teaching ecology at a university, so that he could translate for me. I could tell that he had been working hard on his English and that he had been studying his Bible. He had a great hunger for God. I noticed that he was no longer just translating for me. He was also partnering with me in ministering to others. I could sense his burden for the people we spoke to.

We walked all over the city together, following up new believers and helping them to get grounded in the gospel. We went to schools and met with teachers and students. We generally started at 10 a.m. and we didn't return until 10 p.m. All day long he was taking notes on English words and Bible verses I had shared with people. Sometimes he would stop me in the middle of a conversation with a person and ask me for clarification on a word or a truth. He couldn't learn enough. I'd never met a man who was more teachable than Roman.

We traveled together by train and by bus to other cities in a neighboring region called Primorsky. We had endless spiritual discussions. Once when we were traveling by train from Khabarovsk to Vladivostok, we were sitting in a compartment with a man and a woman who seemed very sorrowful. I asked them how they were doing and the husband replied that they had just lost their son, a fireman, in an accident. With Roman translating, I tried reaching out to them. I knew what it was like to lose a child. I tried to share the gospel, but they did not want to hear it. They refused any kind of comfort, insisting it was their obligation to mourn their loss for the rest of their lives.

Roman was as deeply grieved as I was for them. He could see how hopeless and pained people are without Christ in their lives. We shared that burden. As we ministered together, we also shared an anointing that God had given to us. I knew then that he was the man I had been asking God to give me.

Roman started attending a gathering in Khabarovsk that was forming into a church. Many people came just searching for the truth. Some trusted Christ but then would not return. No one was helping them grow in their faith. This disturbed Roman. He was accustomed to counseling people along with me. He yearned to see people growing in relation to Christ. It was obvious to me that, in Roman, God was forming a good shepherd for His people.

For three years I went regularly to Russia. At first I went for three months at a time, returning home for three months, and then returning again. That got to be too much for both Jeanette and me. I spread out my trips to a more manageable level. Jeanette went with me on three occasions. Our daughter, Deb, went with me once. It was great to have them along to share with the women. Plus, they both shared the same spirit of prayer, and I was grateful for that. But during her third trip to Russia, Jeanette started having health problems. Her blood pressure went way up. With the fast pace and long hours I kept, it was hard for her to keep up with me. I wore her out. But I could never wear out her heart for praying for me and the work God had called me to do in Russia.

Staff and church members from Southwest Bible also started coming with me. I recognized the value of the various gifts God has given to that body. It was also obvious that the Lord Himself was doing the recruiting, so I could just relax and be myself again.

Meanwhile, Roman's hunger for God's Word kept increasing. The Baptist Union offered him a scholarship to study at a seminary in St. Petersburg, which is on the opposite side of Russia from Khabarovsk. He spent three years there before returning to Khabarovsk, where he became the pastor of the church he had previously attended. He was obviously God's man in God's place. The church is now called The Transformation Church. God is blessing Roman's ministry and it is continuing to grow.

Along with the spread of the gospel in Russia, many bad influences came into the country from the West. Cults that originated in America found inroads into Russia. With no other basis for discerning spiritual truth, the newly formed Russian government rejoined with the Orthodox Church to flush out unwelcome religions. To do this, an edict was given that no religious group would be officially recognized that had not been documented prior to 1987. This left out the cults, but it also eliminated a lot of solid biblical groups.

I met a man named Yuri in Vladivostok who had a real zeal for reaching people in Primorsky with the gospel. He had researched some old government archives and had discovered that there were three Baptist churches in the area that had been documented under Stalin's regime, although they had been greatly persecuted. But the records proved their validity according to the new edict. So he reformed them into a union called PAMCEC, a Russian acronym for the unified churches in Primorsky, and it was officially recognized. Other churches in Primorsky were added to the group. I recognized Yuri's heart for the gospel as well as his administrative mind. He invited me to work with him in grounding the churches in the Word. This gave me an official connection with the churches in Russia.

I went with Yuri to visit several of the PAMCEC churches. Driving in Russia is a notoriously dangerous ordeal. Yuri was a terrific driver, but like most vehicles in Eastern Russia, his car was Japanese-made, which meant the steering wheel is situated on the right side. But as in America, the flow of traffic on the road is also on the right lane. This means that when a driver wants to pass a slow-moving vehicle, he needs to swerve into the oncoming lane to get a view of what's ahead. This is also true of the other drivers on the road. They too must swerve into the oncoming lane to see what's coming. This is why driving in Russia can be a dangerous ordeal. I saw the aftermath of some horrible accidents along the roads.

Yuri and I were driving up a long hill toward sunset and a car ahead of us was just chugging along. Yuri's windshield was dirty, so it was hard for him to see through it with the sun reflecting on the glass. I was sitting on the left side, which gave me the clear view of the road ahead. I noticed Yuri inching toward the left side of the road like he was going to pass. He was accelerating and passing when suddenly a truck came barreling at us out of nowhere. It was too late for me to say anything but, "Jesus!" I meant it as a prayer.

Yuri's reflexes took over. He squeezed his car between the car beside him and the oncoming truck, which veered only slightly to the side. We could hear the side of Yuri's car scraping the vehicle he was passing. Yuri quickly pulled to the side of the road and I could see him trembling. We both just sat there in complete silence with our stomachs in our throats. I didn't know what to say. The driver of the car we had passed pulled over behind us to look at the damage. Amazingly, there wasn't a scratch on either vehicle, even though we had heard them scraping.

Afterward, Yuri and I sat in silence for a long time, parked along the highway. We were both praying, thanking God for His protection. After about fifteen minutes I looked at Yuri and said, "I am fully supportive of you."

Yuri sat thinking for a while longer and then he said, "John, if you see anything in my life that you think needs to change, I will listen to you."

I knew then that God had given me another key man in Russia.

24
The Russian Road

Through the years, I kept going back and forth to Eastern Russia as often as I could, but I always felt concerned that the believers there needed a consistent diet of sound biblical teaching. Coming from America once or twice a year, I was not in a position to give it to them. I met many sincere, dear followers of Jesus in those little churches that were scattered among the Primorsky region. The churches were still in their infancy, struggling to survive with few to feed them from the Word. I had learned from my work in Ethiopia and Liberia that the door of opportunity can close swiftly, so it was critical to develop leaders who could lovingly guide them into the knowledge of God's grace and truth in Christ. I always felt a sense of urgency about it.

Russia's long history of autocratic leadership made it challenging to develop spiritual leaders. The men didn't have many models of leaders who were kind and able to give wise counsel. Many leaders in the culture were corrupt and demanding. When a man with leadership capabilities came to Christ, he usually let go of his corrupt ways, but his demanding ways were more difficult to let go. It was the only way he knew how to keep control. I think this was tied to the broken relationships between fathers and sons, as much as it was to the model of leadership in the culture. Yuri once told me, "John, I have never had a father-figure in my life until now. You are my father-figure."

Just as I had done in Africa, I arranged three-day Bible teaching conferences among PAMCEC churches throughout Primorsky. Southwest Bible Church sent over teams of teachers. The Russian believers came from far and wide, cramming themselves into vans, to attend the meetings. They were spiritually hungry. Along with our teaching sessions, we spent many hours personally counseling believers who were struggling with all kinds of hurts and difficulties.

Oleg, a pastor of a small church in Vladivostok, was one of our drivers. He soaked up the teaching along with everybody else. He also sat in on many counseling sessions, along with a translator. He told me, "John, I like watching how you talk with the people. I am learning a lot from you."

Oleg is a huge man with a heart as big as his frame. I could sense that he cared deeply for people and he was sincerely seeking to know and follow Christ. It was clear to me that God wanted me to invest in his life. Knowing that he was always watching me, I tried to make every minute count that I had with him. Every moment was a teachable moment.

One lady apologized to me after I had counseled her in some personal problems she was facing. She told me, "I am sorry you had to spend so much of your time with me."

I told her, "I don't spend time, I invest time." This may sound trite, but it is true. We don't know how much time we will have here on the earth, and it might be less than we think. God hasn't given us time to either spend or waste. He gives it to us to invest. By investing my time, I mean making the most of every opportunity the Lord gives me to help another person learn to know Him. I always thought, even if I am not the best Bible scholar or teacher or language learner, I can still work my hardest with what God has given to me to use in serving Him. All I wanted to do was to make Him known. So I figured every person He brought my way was a divine appointment.

Sometimes divine appointments come by surprise. I brought a group of personal evangelists along with me to Russia on one occasion. By personal evangelists, I mean those who are gifted in speaking one-on-one with people about the Lord. Like believers everywhere, the Russians needed to learn how to effectively communicate the gospel. We organized personal evangelism conferences in several towns. On this particular trip, our final conference was held in Vladivostok in one of the largest evangelical churches in the city. There was a large turnout.

I planned to guide the people through a presentation of the gospel called the line diagram, so I asked for a volunteer to play the role of an unbeliever. A lady promptly stood up and walked forward and onto the stage. I told her I wanted her to respond to me as though she were an unbeliever. She said, "Yes, I am an unbeliever."

I did not understand what she meant. I thought she meant that she was agreeing to play this role. My translator, Zhenya, understood what she meant. She meant that she actually was not a believer. Zhenya quickly tried to explain this to me, but I still didn't get it. I was too intent on demonstrating how to lead a person to faith in Christ.

But the people watching understood what was happening and they began praying for us. I went through the entire gospel with her, asking her questions along the way to be sure she understood, as I always do. She went right along with me, nodding and saying she understood. After I had explained the gospel to her, I wanted to

Ludmila coming to faith

show the people how to lead a person in a prayer to express their desire to invite Christ into their heart. I led the volunteer lady through a prayer expressing her need for forgiveness and giving a summary of what Christ had done for her on the cross. She prayed along with me, uttering every word of the prayer. When I looked up at her, I could see that her face was beaming. The people started cheering and applauding. This woman had actually come to faith in Christ before my very eyes, and I was the last to realize it.

This made quite an impression on the people. They saw firsthand that people are hungry for God, but they need someone to show them how to find him. If God could use me in my ignorance, he could use them in theirs also.

It was the kind of impression I was especially trying to make on the pastors. It came by design, not by accident. I wanted them to see that every person is important to the Lord, and so it is important to treat everyone with love and respect. It doesn't take a Bible scholar to lead a person to trust in Christ. It only takes one person with a hungry heart and another person who is simply available to God, to be used by Him for His glory.

While I tried to demonstrate this to the men I was investing in, I also wanted the translators to feel that they were as valuable to me and to the Lord as the people we were communicating with. I couldn't have done anything without their help. And the Lord provided us with some very good translators.

In my early days in Russia, a teacher named Lena translated for me. Roman came along a little later on and then came a young man named Renat. Like Roman, he was self-taught in English. He was very bright and eager to learn more about the Lord. I had hoped that he would become another Roman, leading a church, but he went instead into business and became a very effective personal evangelist among his customers.

Yuri's daughter, Inna, helped translate for us, along with some of her wonderful friends: Ira, Nastya, Anna and Zhenya, who translated for me when I unexpectedly led that woman to the Lord by divine appointment. These translators became like daughters to me. Like all new believers, they struggled to grasp truth and live out what we were teaching, but they served us eagerly and they learned with grateful, teachable hearts. And like the people we counseled, they had their own personal struggles too. But they took time away from their families to help us. They often wept with the people we were trying to help, while they were translating. It is a difficult mental job, especially translating for me, because I pushed them through long hours every day. Then if you add to it the emotionally draining effects of listening to the deep hurts of people, it is extremely wearing. At the end of each long demanding day, they fell asleep exhausted.

Many of my translators became like daughters to me.

Zhenya's grandmother, Nena, was among the first to follow Christ. She was a humble, quiet woman, full of wisdom and kindness. Jeanette loved being with her. They couldn't understand each other's language, but they shared the same love for the Lord and the same quiet spirit. I sometimes felt that words would probably just get in the way of a good conversation between those two ladies.

Nena's daughter, Dalia, shared the same sweet spirit, and I could see the same in her daughter, Zhenya. It was wonderful to see three generations of joyful Russian believers. At that time this was a rare sight, but having seen it happen in my own family, I wanted to see it happening in families all over Russia. When the love of God is shed from one generation to another down family lines, from one family to the next, eventually a whole nation can be changed and blessed for the glory of God.

But none of that could happen if the people were not being taught from God's Word. I heard about a pastor from Ukraine who was an excellent Bible expositor who had a church in Battleground, Washington. His name is Alexey. His church is just across the Columbia River from my home in Oregon, so I visited the church along with a friend from Southwest Bible, Pete Smith. When we visited, Alexey was teaching through the Gospel of Matthew in Russian, which was then translated into English. I was very impressed by his teaching. He was in chapter ten and he had been teaching from the book for several months. I knew this was the kind of thorough teaching that would benefit the churches of Primorsky. I purchased some CDs of his messages and I asked for permission to duplicate them for the churches in Eastern Russia.

I took ten of Alexey's CD recordings along with me on my next trip to Russia. As it happened, Yuri knew Alexey. So he highly recommended his teaching to the pastors who were under the PAMCEC umbrella. At first, the pastors seemed hesitant to receive teaching on a CD. It was all very new to them. They didn't even have Christian radio, so they weren't sure what to make of using technology as a teaching tool. But one by one, pastors began to let down their guard. Eventually it really caught on. None of the pastors had been taught how to do expository teaching. But they were encouraged by Alexey's teaching, and they shared his messages with the people in their churches. I saw, even more clearly, how useful and edifying technology can be in equipping God's people for service. But I had yet to see how greatly God would use a simple device, called an MP3, to connect my work in

Russia to the work I had left behind in Africa. The way back to Africa was still ahead of me.

Alexey invited Yuri to his church in Washington and then asked him to accompany him to a pastor's conference at Grace Community Church in California, where John MacArthur is pastor. Alexey had been trained under MacArthur's teaching at The Master's Seminary. Not only was the teaching terrific, but Yuri was also greatly encouraged by the model of ministry he experienced there. The entire staff at Grace Community constantly served the visiting pastors, modeling to them the reality of servant leadership.

Not long afterward, Alexey started a pastor's training school in Ukraine. He wanted to pass along the method of Bible teaching and the philosophy of ministry he had learned under MacArthur. This was the kind of training the Russian pastors needed, so I asked the leadership at Southwest Bible if they would help send two pastors there for a two-week teaching module. They were glad to do so. I raised more funds to help others go also. During my eighteen years of serving the Lord in Russia, this was one of the most significant investments I made in the lives of these men.

As with time, money is not intended to be spent or wasted. It is meant to be invested, and there is no better investment than God's people who are being prepared by Him to do His work.

25
The Way Back Home

During a trip to Russia in the summer of 2001, I started having trouble with my hip. It hurt so badly I could barely get around with a cane. When I returned home, I decided to get it checked out, thinking it was probably my bad back acting up again, radiating pain down to my hip. It was September when I finally got an appointment with my doctor. I already had a plane ticket for the next trip back to Russia. But after my hip was X-rayed, the news I got from the doctor put a sudden stop to all my plans.

When the doctor told me I had multiple myeloma, he gave me a five-year prognosis. Cancer makes war in your body. It had eaten a hole in my hip the size of a baseball. I had already been forced out of two countries by wars. Now with this new war raging in my body, it looked like I might be taken out again.

We gathered as a family to pray. My first response was to give thanks to God. I became genuinely excited about going to heaven soon. I could identify with the Apostle Paul when, facing death, he said, *"to depart and be with Christ is better by far."*[18]

But then I started feeling torn. What about my family and friends and the many people I had given myself to for the sake of the gospel? I had a strong conviction that God had more for me yet to do. So I could also identify with Paul's other statement: *"but it is more necessary for you that I remain in the body."*[19]

I didn't have control over how long I would live, but I did have a say in *how* I would live the rest of my days. I decided to live as I had always done. I chose to fight for my life. This meant undergoing grueling rounds of chemo and radiation treatments, bone infusions and two stem cell transplants. I had to take pain medicine that made me so groggy I could hardly think. So I took as low a dosage as I could, just enough to take the bite off the pain. I wanted to be clear in the head so I could focus on Jeanette and my daughters and my grandchildren, as well as the doctors and nurses and everyone else the Lord put in my path. Cancer helped me to rearrange my personal priorities.

I spent more time praying than I ever did before. I couldn't be constantly on the go anymore, so I simply had more time to pray. But I also longed to spend more time in God's presence. My soul yearned for Him.

I also started listening more to people. I had never been much of a listener, but I started listening in a new way to Jeanette and the girls. I began hearing their concerns without interrupting to give them a quick fix. When you are living with a problem of your own that doesn't have a quick fix you begin to understand that others have problems that can't be fixed, just like that. I've heard it said that cancer can actually be good for you. I don't recommend it, but I do think it has caused me to become more patient and more caring.

Gradually I started feeling better. After a year of treatments, the doctor said I had gone into remission. I felt renewed. I was determined to strengthen the muscles around my hip, so I bought a ten-speed bicycle and started riding everywhere I could. Some of my friends from Southwest Bible were surprised to see me riding from our home in the outskirts of Portland to the downtown area and back again. That was over twenty miles round-trip. I rode there on Wednesdays to witness with some of the folks who attended Downtown Bible Class, where Scott Gilchrist was teaching.

I also bought a rowboat. I enjoyed loading the grandkids into it and rowing and fishing on a lake. I hadn't taken time to do stuff like that in years. It was good learning how to have fun again.

When cancer goes into remission, it's like a ceasefire in war. You never know when the battle might flare up again. I was feeling better, so in 2002 I took another trip to Russia. I was glad to return there, but I was also keeping a close eye on what was happening in Liberia.

One day I was surprised to get a letter from Morris Barwor, a guy in Liberia who I figured had been killed in the war. Morris had written to me from a refugee camp in Sierra Leone, where he had fled for safety along with his wife and children and thousands of other Liberians. It took eight months for his letter to reach me via the Red Cross and SIM headquarters. I wrote back to him and arranged to have him call me. As we talked on the phone, Morris described some of the atrocities he had seen and he told me about what had happened to many believers we knew in Liberia during Taylor's reign of terror. As far as he could tell, about thirty believers we had personally known had been either killed or had died in the forests while hiding from Taylor's forces. Some had died from sickness and others had starved to death.

By 2003, UN forces in Liberia were pushing Taylor's forces away from Monrovia and further back into the countryside. Thinking my cancer was possibly now behind me for the time-being, I began to believe there could still be a way for me to return there some day. I started praying and making plans for my return.

Through my phone calls with Morris, I sensed that God had deeply matured and strengthened him since I had last seen him. He told me the story of how God had been working in his life.

Morris was a teenage boy when I met him shortly after we came to Kolahun. But even then I could see there was something special about him. He had trusted Christ and I recognized that he was very sincere, unlike many of the others who were living double lives. He kept coming to me, asking questions about the Lord. It was all on his initiative. He really wanted to know God. So

I would take him along with me on my motorcycle and we'd go out to the villages together. He was just kind of hanging around with me. I didn't necessarily see him as a potential leader at the time. I just saw him as a sincere young man who wanted to be my sidekick.

But he was very bright and he often translated for me. He also helped me to improve my cultural awareness. Sometimes I would say something that wasn't very culturally sensitive, and Morris would correct me. Most of the Liberians seemed to be afraid to correct a white person, but he wasn't afraid to tell me when I was making a mistake. So Morris became my teacher. I appreciated his help.

I wasn't formally discipling him. It was just life-on-life. When I was ministering to people he would watch me, and I would explain the Scriptures to him when a question came up. It was all very natural. I felt like a father speaking to his son. Morris opened up to me about all kinds of life struggles and I was able to help him. Because he was still so young, I didn't recognize him as a key leader. But God knew the plan He had for Morris, and He knew what it would take to forge him into one of His key men in Liberia.

ELWA needed a good Gbandi broadcaster, so after Morris graduated from high school, I recommended they hire him. While he was working there he also attended a Bible college. As he learned to know God through His Word, his desire to serve Him kept increasing. I connected with him often when I went down to Monrovia. It was a joy to see him growing in the knowledge of the Lord.

When the war forced the missionaries from Liberia and ELWA was shut down, Morris had nowhere to go except back to Kolahun. By then he was married with children. He took his family through the treacherous countryside and found his way back home. With no missionaries around to help him, Morris started about forty fellowship groups in the villages in the area. He served as pastor to the people. He also took many war-orphaned children into his home. Some of the fellowships he started were among the Muslim people who lived in the southern Gbandi region. None of us missionaries had ever seen that kind of fruitfulness in ministry.

In 2001, Taylor's forces headed north from Monrovia to counter opposing forces. Kolahun was caught in the middle of the fighting. Taylor's men were murderous gangs. They raped and ransacked everywhere, killing people on sight. Five of our church leaders were killed. People fled through the forests seeking refuge in Sierra Leone or in Guinea. Morris and his family escaped to Sierra Leone where they found refuge in a Red Cross camp. That is where he was staying when he wrote his letter to me.

But by then, Taylor's days were numbered in Monrovia. A UN coalition finally forced him out in 2003. There were still forces loyal to Taylor upcountry, but he was brought to trial for war crimes at the World Court in The Hague. I heard reports that Monrovia was quiet, so I purchased a plane ticket. I had also personally met with former Portland police chief Mark Kroeker, who was now heading the security police in Liberia. When I arrived in Monrovia, he allowed me to ride by special UN convoy all the way through the rebel territory to the refugee camps in Sierra Leone. Along the way, I was stunned by the destruction and the distress I could see, but I was also overwhelmed by God's grace and provision in allowing me to return to Liberia.

I had a joyous reunion with Morris. We connected through the Red Cross. He led me to about ten refugee camps where we held open-air Bible conferences. The people crowded together. At one of the camps, I was so grateful to reunite with Hena. He had planned to leave the camp to head home to Fassavolo but the Lord cautioned him to wait one more day. I thanked the Lord that we didn't miss each other and that Hena and his wife were still alive. I still had the Scripture verse in my wallet that Jeanette had found on our attic floor in Kolahun: *"Be still and know that I am God: I will be exalted among the heathen, I will be exalted in the earth."*[20] I still keep it there to remind me that God's promises are true no matter what is happening in me or in the world.

My body had been wearing down from the demands of the journey, and I got a bad case of pneumonia. I wound up in a clinic

Staying at Morris' refugee house for five nights

at a refugee camp for a few days. This would be the first of many bouts of pneumonia I have had. I lost count at seventeen, plus seven cases of shingles.

After I got back on my feet, I was able to take Morris and a few others with me back to Kolahun. We went to our property where I had built our home. The land was so overgrown, we had to cut our way through to the house, using a machete. The whole building had crumbled down to its cement foundation, leaving only a broken wall around the perimeter of the building. Trees and bushes had grown up inside the area where our house used to stand.

As we sat there on the wall, I looked at the war-weary faces of those men. They had suffered the loss of their own homes and many loved ones during the war. They could see that we had suffered loss as well. But we started giving thanks to God for taking us through it all, worshiping Him for the great things He had done.

The whole nation of Liberia lay in ruins like that tangled mess which had once been our home. My body was also a tangled mess, ravaged by cancer and by illness that had invaded it like a brutal army. I still wouldn't say that cancer is good for you, any more than war is good for a nation. But I can say that God uses these evil things to bring about His good purposes. Knowing this has helped me to be still and praise Him.

Sitting on the ruins of our Kolahun house
with Morris and others

26
Building on the Ruins

Our crumbled house in Kolahun was like a picture of how quickly war can destroy the things we put our heart into building. If I had tried to rebuild it, it would have needed to be bulldozed and started all over again. It didn't have a solid base to build on. After the war, the church in Liberia was in about the same shape as our house. It was nearly destroyed. The best way to rebuild it was by starting over, laying a new foundation. The old foundation on which it stood was too weak.

That's because the church's old foundation was generally a mixture of tribal beliefs blended with some hazy biblical thinking and a lot of superstition. No wonder it couldn't withstand the storm. Many believers were standing on shaky ground to start with. When they were able to regroup, some of their leaders, with the exception of Morris Barwor and Hena, started taking them back to their old ways.

The weakness in the church was mostly due to a lack of biblical training. It wasn't for lack of sincerity. The war had purged a lot of hypocrisy from the church.

I was at a church conference in Monrovia where a very eloquent pastor was speaking. He was a highly-educated man with a degree from a prestigious university. He was talking about how he spiritually prepared himself for delivering a message on

Sundays. He said there was sometimes friction between him and his wife on a Saturday evening. So he described a bathing routine they did during the daytime to cleanse themselves from all the bad vibes that came between them at night. This, he said, did the trick. It lifted all the tension in the home.

I sat there thinking, *what is he talking about?*

I realized that he was actually describing a tribal cleansing practice to ward off the effects of evil spirits. In following this occult practice, he was unintentionally honoring demons. Seeking to be free from the power of demons, he was naively subjecting himself and his family to the fear of demons. So then, what was he exposing the church to with this kind of instruction? I thought, *Here this guy has all that education. He has the skill to speak. He has leadership abilities. But he doesn't know the Scriptures. He needs sound biblical training.*

So I approached him as a brother who is caught in an error. I spoke to him kindly and directly saying, "You are giving way to demons by showing them respect. God says you are not to fear them; you shall fear only the Lord."

He was very thankful that I had warned him against acting in this way, but he still didn't know how to change. I could see that he was humble and teachable. He wanted to do well. I wondered how I could help him to build a better foundation for his faith and his church.

Before Scott Gilchrist teaches or preaches from any book of the Bible, he reads it fifty times, and then he copies it with his own hand. This is his proven way of saturating his mind with a book so that its message penetrates his heart and enables him to teach it in clear terms. The truth of it just oozes out of him.

During that conference I had been teaching from Philippians. I thought, if I asked this pastor to read through Philippians fifty times, it would be too overwhelming, so I advised him to read it just twenty times. I told him he should then copy the book, one chapter a day, until he had copied the entire book. This pastor thought it was a good idea and he thanked me for it. Philippians is a good book for getting a good look at the face of Christ in the

Scriptures. I could see that he wasn't really very familiar with Jesus, at least not in his experience. He was letting his own experiences, rather than God's Word, color his interpretation of Jesus. This had led him to some mistaken conclusions and some unbiblical practices. Later after following this plan, he told me, "I just love Philippians because now I know what it is talking about. I love every verse in it because I now understand the context behind it."

I sensed that he was realizing the life-changing power of the Word. He didn't need me to lecture him about what he was doing wrong. His action was actually a symptom of his wrong thinking, which only the Word could correct. He needed me to help him get started by building a right foundation for his faith on the Word.

I saw the same problem in the church all over Liberia. The leaders had not been trained in the Word. Many of them got up in front of people on a Sunday morning and just said whatever came to mind, maybe sprinkled with some verses from the Bible. It had been that way before the war, and it was bound to be repeated if pastors didn't get grounded in the Word.

Despite my health challenges, I've made several return visits to Liberia. I wound up with pneumonia a few more times, which waylaid me in crusty clinics in remote places like Kolahun for several days. But, knowing I don't have a lot of time left in this world has motivated me to do all I can, as long as I can.

Around that time, I also gathered a shipping container full of books discarded from the Beaverton, Reynolds and Evergreen school districts in Oregon and Washington to ship out to Liberia. This was to aid the public schools and the seminary that had been ransacked and neglected through the war. My older grandkids helped me sort and pack the books for the container.

In 2005, radio ELWA was just getting back up and running again. I inquired what it would take to get Scott Gilchrist's teaching on the radio there. I had previously handed out some cassette tapes with his teaching, and the Liberian pastors liked the way he spoke in such clear, understandable tones. He didn't talk too fast for them. Nor did he use a lot of illustrations or colloquialisms that didn't make sense in Liberian culture. Scott is plainspoken and his teaching is easy to follow because he goes verse-by-verse through each book that he teaches.

It would take just $400 per month to get Scott on ELWA five nights a week. When I discussed this idea with the Southwest Bible leadership, they said it was a no-brainer. They were happy to get behind it.

Everywhere I went in Liberia, pastors and believers told me how glad they were to listen to Scott's messages on the radio. He was becoming a familiar voice among believers there. Some pastors told me, "I listen to him every day."

I was glad to play a part in getting good teaching to their listening ears, but I knew that listening to good teaching is not enough. The Word needed to dwell deeply inside their hearts if they were to bear lasting fruit that brings glory to God.

So I came back to the idea of reading, rereading and copying Scriptures. One advantage of using this method in Liberia is that they have already been taught this way in the schools. They learn by rote. They just copy a lesson off a blackboard and memorize it. So, copying the Scripture is not as tedious to the Liberian as it might seem to an American. The bigger challenge is to get them to read a book twenty times.

According to an article I read in the *Evangelical Missionary Quarterly*, in 2004 there were 2.2 million evangelical churches in the world. The article stated that only 15 percent of those churches had biblically-trained leaders. In Africa, the percentage is even lower than that. I knew exactly how many pastors in Kolahun had been theologically trained. Zero! If all the evangelical seminaries in the world were operating at 120 percent capacity, they still could not train even ten percent of those untrained leaders.

Very few pastors in Liberia were financially able to go away to a Bible school. They would need to leave their wife and family and farm. But I began to consider that there was perhaps a simpler solution. Maybe the Lord had an answer hidden in plain sight.

There is no better source of theology in the Bible than the Book of Romans. In all of my teaching, I have always insisted that my students start and stay there awhile. It is the book of books, unfolding the message of the gospel clearly. I've always told people, "Read Romans regularly." I didn't originate that decree. It is just a basic maxim for all believers. There is no better doctrinal foundation to build upon. Learn Romans and you will have a good knowledge of God's righteousness and how a person can be made right with God through trusting in what He has done for us in Jesus Christ.

I began encouraging pastors to read Romans twenty times and to write it out by hand. A Liberian pastor named Theophilus did this. To aid his understanding, I gave him a cassette recording with Scott Gilchrist teaching from Romans. His comment was very enlightening to me. He told me he still had a hard time understanding Romans even after reading it twenty times and copying it. "But when I listened to Scott explaining it," he said, "I started to understand what I had read. But I wouldn't have really understood Scott's teaching if I hadn't already read it and copied it myself."

Another pastor named Jeremiah told me he didn't get as much from the taped teaching as he did from his own reading and copying from Romans.

Either way, I understood that people need both the Holy Spirit's guidance and a Spirit-filled teacher to guide them into a clear understanding of the truth. That's when it occurred to me that I should give pastors both a challenge and a reward. The challenge was to read Romans twenty times and also copy it. The reward was an exhaustive collection of Scott's teachings from Romans and many other books of the Bible.

About that time, MP3-players were first coming out. They were expensive at first, costing about $200 apiece, and the technology was still a little rough. But I found I could easily store more than 800 of Scott's messages on each player. He has 125 messages from Romans alone.

I gave a few of these to some guys who had finished the challenge, but I was disappointed to hear that the players didn't last very long. In a few years the technology vastly improved and the price dropped to about $30 per player. I started loading them in a suitcase when I took my return-trips to Liberia. I also added rechargeable batteries and small solar panels. Even at that low price, I knew that ninety-five percent of the pastors could not afford to buy one from me. The only way they could get one was if I gave it to them. But I didn't want to just give them away. I had gone through that before with believers just wanting me to give them something without any cost to themselves. I didn't want to reinforce that old "gimme" mentality that was so rampant among believers before the war. I wanted them to value the MP3's by earning one. So I promised an MP3 to any leader who read Romans twenty times and copied it out by hand. This became known as the Romans Project.

Beginning of the Romans Project

I challenged a seminary student named Elijah to read Romans fifty times and copy it by hand. I knew the seminary he attended didn't put any extra emphasis on studying Romans, so I gave him an emphasis of my own. When he had completed the challenge, I gave him an MP3 with Scott's teaching from the Bible. After digesting the Scriptures he had read and copied, and then listening to the messages from Romans, Elijah told me it was like a new book to him. He said the seminary seemed like nothing to him now. He told me, "Now I really understand the gospel."

I mention this not to demean seminary training, but to demonstrate the power of understanding that the Holy Spirit opens to any person who uses this simple method. It is so simple, hiding in plain sight all along.

The Romans Project doesn't stop with reading, writing and studying Romans. I have recommended that pastors and leaders also read and copy First Timothy, and then listen to Scott's teaching, so they can understand church order. I counsel them to do the same with Second Timothy, so they will know how to handle disorder in the church. Titus spells out the qualifications for leaders in the church. In fact, going through all the books of the Bible, from Genesis to Revelation, is essential. The Romans Project offers a comprehensive plan for filling the mind with Scripture, rendering the man of God profitable for every good work.

I'm sure that MP3 players are getting more commonplace in Africa as it catches up with the technology of the rest of the world, but until now it has been a thing of status to own one. More church leaders want to have one. As word spread, it soon became a challenge to keep up with the demand. One pastor would see another one listening in on his MP3 and he'd ask, "What is that thing in your ear? How can I get one?"

But the MP3 player alone has not been the selling point. The real attraction is the way that pastors have benefited from filling their minds and hearts with the Word. It is transforming lives and whole churches.

The Evangelical Churches Union of Liberia selected a Gbandi pastor named Momo to work with me in getting their leaders involved with the Romans Project. He is the pastor of the

International Church in Monrovia. Momo faithfully ministered among his people through the war and he saw the need to help other leaders get established in the Word. We became close very quickly, kindred hearts in the Lord. I loved his heart for God and I could see that he was yet another one of God's key men.

27
A Focus on My Family

Jeanette has often said, "What shall it profit a mother if she gain the whole world but lose her own kids?" This has been her passion – that her own kids would know the Lord. She helped me to focus on this purpose also. When we lived in Africa, I was constantly ministering outside the home, so it could have been easy for me to pass the responsibility to her for seeing that our own kids were being raised in the ways of the Lord. But Jeanette was very mindful of how quickly kids grow up and go to college and then go off into the rest of their lives. When our girls were at home from boarding school, she made sure we set aside one day a week just to be with them.

Jeanette is now reaping the benefits of all the time and devotion she gave to our girls. As grown women with children of their own, each of the girls still loves being with her mom and they love being with each other.

Now as grandparents, we would say the same thing about our grandkids. If our grandkids were going the wrong way, I think we would have missed the other most important assignment the Lord has given us to do. Thankfully, we are blessed to have great relationships with them too. Our daughters' children are great friends. All of the cousins love to hang out with each other.

My dad used to quote Exodus 20:5,6, which is talking about God's action in the lives of future generations, a trickle down effect because of an individual's response to God. *"...I, the LORD your God, am a jealous God,... showing lovingkindness to thousands, to those who love Me and keep My commandments."*[21] Jeanette and I have eighteen grandchildren. We love every one of them. God loves grandchildren too, but He doesn't have any spiritual grandchildren. Each one has to be born from above by His Spirit through his or her own personal response to Jesus Christ. I have felt the burden to teach them.

Throughout my life and ministry, I have tried to give away the truth and grace the Lord has freely given to me. I have also tried to give away something that I never personally received myself. I never had a personal mentor to guide and help me grow in my relationship with the Lord. My father was a godly man and he was my great example in the faith, but he didn't spend much time alone with me teaching me how to walk with the Lord. He had a radical faith and God used Him mightily. I admired him, but mostly from a distance. Knowing what I had missed out on helped me to understand the importance of personally discipling and mentoring the key men God gave to me in ministry. Many men, especially in Russia, were fatherless and needed an older brother in the faith to guide them. I have learned that my own children and grandchildren have needed the same from me. What would I gain if I won the whole world for Christ and lost my own family along the way?

I was thinking about the importance of passing along the spiritual baton to my grandchildren, so I invited my oldest grandson, Josiah, to have a meal with me at Chang's Mongolian Grill. He was about eighteen at that time. Josiah is a sharp young man with a healthy hunger for God. We have always enjoyed each other's company. So I asked him, "Would you like to regularly meet with me, just to talk and maybe do a little Bible study together?"

His response was encouraging, but not surprising. "Grandpa," he said. "When I was a kid you were always interested in me. You took me fishing and we did all kinds of things together. Why wouldn't I want to do that?"

Several years earlier, when Josiah was ten or eleven, Jeanette and I decided to help him go to a Christian camp during the summer. We agreed to pay half the cost, with his parents, Curt and Melodie, paying the other half. I am a firm believer in not just giving a kid money to do something that they would enjoy doing anyway. I believe in dangling a carrot on a stick to motivate them to earn their way, to help them get even more value from the experience.

I assigned Josiah to read through all but eight chapters in Proverbs. It has a lot of wisdom and instruction for right living in a family atmosphere and for helping a boy grow into a godly man. I instructed him to copy every line, referring to fathers, mothers, children and young men, into a notebook. He then was required to underline each with a different color, indicating a command, a consequence for disobedience, or a resulting blessing of obedience. I told him to also pick out six or more verses that really hit him in the heart, then write those out on separate pieces of paper and put them up on his bedroom wall so he could keep reading them. This he did. His mother told me that when he occasionally got out-of-sorts, Josiah would go to his bedroom and

Playing "Signs" with my grandkids at our yearly family camping trip

get out his notebook and reread it. He would come out a little later and be very civil.

I also came up with odd jobs around our house for him to do. I had him pulling weeds and cutting grass and doing all kinds of odds and ends with me. I had learned the value of hard physical work when I was a boy, and I didn't want him to miss out on the opportunity. This is how Josiah earned his way to summer camp.

Seeing the fruit of this approach, Jeanette and I started extending the invitation to the rest of the grandchildren. Some of them did character studies from the Old Testament. I had them all reading and copying Scripture. Each kid had to earn his or her own way to summer camp by doing the Bible study, memorizing Scriptures and doing practical work. This continued on down through the years. I suppose it was one of the things that led toward an interest, on the part of the grandkids, to enter into a Bible study with their grandpa.

Romans is the best book in the Bible for building a life of faith, so that's where I decided to start with Josiah. We began the study and eventually it grew to eight grandchildren. I could see that the kids were growing in the Lord. They have read Romans a number of times and have copied it, kind of like the pastors in Africa are doing. It has had the same faith-enriching effect on them.

To prepare the Israelites to go into the Promised Land, God gave Moses this command: *You, your children and their children after them must fear the Lord your God as long as you live.* [22] At this point, we're up to chapter 14 in our Romans study. It's been going on for about four years. I don't know how much farther I can take them, but I am counting on the older cousins to influence the younger ones when I am gone.

Spending this time together in the Word has boosted their confidence for reaching out to their peers. Michael asked me to help him start a Bible study among his high school buddies. So until I got sick again, on Wednesday mornings I drove over to meet with him and his friends before school. The other grandkids are also growing.

One of the best developments from this study is the closeness we share together. They like to come over to Grandpa and Grandma's house and just hang out with us. Sometimes one of them will call me up and say, "Grandpa, can I come over and just talk with you?"

This is one of the best gifts I could ever want – to be so close to my grandchildren that they want to spend time with me.

One of the problems with my cancer is that I can't hug my grandkids anymore. Due to my weak immune system, I can't fight off a common cold. I've always loved to tickle the little ones, but I can't do that either. So they started feeling uncertain about how to relate to me. Some started giving me a little nudge on the side. It made the relationship a little warmer.

To get more concentrated time with the older grandkids, I rented a cabin for a three-day weekend so we could go over our study in Romans. I wanted to make sure they were all heading in the right direction.

The Romans Project with my grandkids

I couldn't have been more pleased with them. They all had a great attitude about serving each other. Twice a day we worked through a section of Romans. Before each session we had a time of worship. We had some great discussions and we also had some good times of getting outside riding bikes. It was challenging for big bodies to ride a small bike with knees protruding around the low handle bars, but we all had lots of laughs doing it. The kids all said that weekend away with Grandpa made Romans more real to them. It made an impression on them that they would always remember.

Jeanette and I pray every morning before breakfast for our grandchildren. Sometimes I've been too sick to remember to pray when I've been in the hospital, but I know that she is always praying. The Lord is able to keep them from the evil that is in the schools, so we ask Him to protect them and to help them be a light to those around them. We pray that none of them will be missing from His kingdom due to lusts or the lure of the world. We pray for our daughters and their husbands, that their intimacy with the Lord will be sweet and fresh, and that they will have wisdom to guide their children. I believe God has been answering our prayers.

There was a time when some of our daughters were feeling that I would be most pleased with them if they would also go out as missionaries. When we were all together, I told them, "I don't want you to become a missionary because you think that's what I want you to be. My desire is that you would do whatever God is calling you to do. God must call you and He must lead you."

My dad really impacted me because he was constantly quoting and living by Scripture. He lived and breathed the truth. He had his faults. He could sometimes be too harsh. But there was no duplicity in him. He was an authentic Christian. Through his example, each of his ten children has been involved in various ministries and all are walking with the Lord.

We were all impacted by my parents' faith and obedience to the Lord. They loved the Lord with a simple, radical love. I am thankful for the wonderful heritage I received from them and I have tried to pass the same legacy to our children and grandchildren. They are also benefiting from the spiritual breakthrough my parents made in our family line. Whatever they may do to serve Him is pleasing to me, but my greatest joy is to hear and see that our daughters, their husbands and our grandchildren are walking in the truth. Jeanette and I have done the best we could to help them grow in the knowledge of the Lord. To hear Him say to me, "Well done, good and faithful servant" for leading my family to Him, this will be my greatest reward in heaven.

28

He Carries Me

Until I got cancer, I didn't fully grasp the Apostle Paul's response to God's message to him: *"My grace is sufficient for you, for power is perfected in weakness."*[23]

In response, Paul wrote, *"I will rather boast about my weaknesses, so that the power of Christ may dwell in me."*[24]

Weakness was something I seldom talked about, much less boasted about. I didn't deny that I had some obvious weaknesses. But I was also determined to be faithful in ministry. I was single-minded. This was my strength. Then cancer showed me that I was actually much weaker than I knew.

When I was first diagnosed in 2001, God gave me a promise: *"For I am the LORD your God, who upholds your right hand, who says to you, 'Do not fear, I will help you.'"*[25]

I came to treasure these words. But I didn't know how badly I needed His help until every hour became a trial. Cancer has convinced me that I desperately need Him, even for my next breath. It has also taught me that my time on earth is not measured by the tick of a clock, but by what I make of the opportunities God has given me. I have learned to savor every moment. Each and every breath I get has turned into a gift from God.

Pain weakens a person's will to live. Many people give up hope and stop trying when pain gets a stranglehold on them. I tried fighting through the pain and resisting my weakness. I was determined to glorify God in my fight, but resisting only made me weaker. Then the Lord told me not to resist my weakness, but to rest in it. That is when I discovered His strength. Not in resisting, but in resting. By resting in my own weakness, realizing that I had no power to withstand my illness, I rested in His daily, moment-by-moment supply of strength. A favorite hymn kept coming to my mind, *"Jesus, I Am Resting, Resting."* I sing it all the time and His praise fills my soul. This is how His power has been perfected in me.

To remove all doubt about who is the real hero of my story, I will freely acknowledge my weaknesses, so that it is evident that He is the source of my strength. By God's grace, I have lived for eleven years with multiple myeloma. Any measure of victory I have seen during my illness belongs to Him. Through it all, His grace has been sufficient for me.

When cancer or any other disease invades your body, it invades much more than that. It invades your whole family. Before my cancer, we had already experienced pain and suffering on a lot of levels. We were well-acquainted with grief. We had lost our little Nathan in Ethiopia. The pain of death is separation. We had also experienced the pain of separation when the kids went off to boarding school and when we had to leave the people we loved due to war. But a shared pain also builds a bond between people who love each other.

So when I came down with cancer, my loving family joined in my suffering. It is a shared pain, felt by me and by Jeanette and by each of our daughters and her family. Each of us has felt it and each of us has dealt with it in our own way. Suffering makes you sensitive to degrees of pain in your body, but it also alerts you to the different ways that people love you. I appreciate those differences in each of my daughters. Each of them possesses a special grace that I take as a gift to me from God. I am glad for how the Lord has expressed His love to me through each of them.

Melodie has always had a heart for others. She shares her mother's gift of mercy. She is always reaching out to someone in need. Melodie will do anything to serve me. I can tell she hurts when she sees me hurting.

Reenie is a creative, loving person. She listens carefully and she tells lively, enjoyable stories. She also prays with a trusting heart. Reenie has a great sense of humor. She helps me to laugh and not take myself so seriously.

Shari is friendly and kind and helpful. She has a warm heart and she makes everyone feel valued. She always puts the needs of others first. Shari notices what needs tending even before I ask for help.

Deb is wise and observant. She is a good counselor. She carefully weighs her words before she speaks. She is also determined, like me. She doesn't back down when it gets hard. Deb is relentlessly loyal to me and to everyone she loves.

Joyce is sweet and joyful. She is also deeply sensitive and caring. Her home is as wide open as her heart. She is everyone's best friend. She always believes the best of me, even in the absence of evidence.

Jeanette is my perfect wife – perfect for me. Even if she had a flaw, I wouldn't tell you about it. Her greatest triumph in life is that she has somehow continued loving me. Her heart is so full of compassion and mercy. I know that God listens intently when she prays. That our family is a very close-knit family, dedicated to Jesus and to one another, is due largely to my wife.

Through the years, I have spent many days and weeks – adding up to months – in the hospital receiving treatments. The hospital has seemed like a second home to me and my family. There have been days when the pain from shingles or neuropathy has been unbearable. I could only lie there praying under my breath, "Jesus. Jesus. Jesus." I was simply asking Him to come into my need at that very moment. In my utter weakness, He was there with me. My body is a temple of His Spirit, so He is also in me. As I was crying out to Him, He let me know that He was near and that He was suffering with me. I felt His presence. His Spirit witnessed to my spirit that He would never leave me. He put a song of praise in my heart:

His Presence Carries You

In all their afflictions, He was afflicted.
In all of their trials, He was tried too.
In all of their sorrows, He bore that sorrow,
And His presence carried them.

In all my afflictions, He is afflicted.
In all of my trials, He is tried too.
In all of my sorrows, He bears that sorrow,
And His presence carries me, yes,
His presence carries me.

In all your afflictions, He is afflicted.
In all of your trials, He is tried too.
In all of your sorrows, He bears that sorrow,
And His presence carries you.

So when you're afflicted, trust Him who's afflicted.
When you are tried, trust Him who's tried too.
When you are in sorrow, trust Him who bears that sorrow,
And His presence will carry you, yes,
His presence will carry you.

During my hospital stays, I have especially enjoyed getting visits from Jeanette and the girls and my grandkids. Some of my good friends have also come to see me. Time and time again my friend, Frank Smith, has driven to pick me up and take me across town to the hospital. The days are long. I greatly enjoy having visitors. After lying in bed for hours, I get restless and need to get a little exercise, so we go walking around the nurses' station with me pushing the "tree" with the IV lines still plugged into my arms. I love singing my song as we go along. I also sing hymns, and some of my visitors are brave enough to join in with me. The cancer ward is generally a joyless place and so I do my best to spread a little joy. The joy of the Lord is still my strength.

Myeloma is a cancer in the immune system that keeps producing mutant rogue cells which attack the cells that are there to fight various diseases. They are like fallen angels inside my immune system. It is non-curable. Some who see me say I look good, but so do rotten apples. The skin doesn't always show what is going on inside the body. Myeloma is essentially painless, but its effects can be very painful.

At one point a tumor started forming between my eyes, causing me to see double. A patch was put over one eye to help the other eye to see better, but it tired quickly when I read. I thought of Hena in Liberia, and how he had gone blind. I felt bonded with him in his suffering. I sympathized with many people I had known in Africa who had suffered far more than me.

The tumor between my eyes was hit with a massive dose of radiation. That treatment restored my vision but it fried my mouth. My tongue was like a raw piece of meat. Drinking water was agonizing. To feed and hydrate myself, I figured out a system for changing the ph balance in my food and beverages. This became a point of interest among the doctors. They asked if I had been a lab technician. I explained that I was a missionary who has had to wing it a lot along the way. Despite my sore tongue, I tried to speak to them about my hope in the Lord. When a doctor asked me how I was doing, I told him, "I'm doing fine, but this body of mine is giving me some trouble." Then I added, "I know where I'm going after my body dies. Do you know where you are going after you die?"

A doctor once told me God doesn't work in the hospital. I couldn't formulate my thoughts because the medication had made my mind foggy. When I later told Deb how I wanted to respond to the doctor, she reminded me that I had already spoken to the doctor about the Lord many times before. She knew the truth. The response was up to her. This encouraged me.

I want so badly to be a witness for Christ in this place where there is no other hope.

Whenever I made my return trips to the hospital, I always tried to be spiritually prepared to be used of God there. I sensed that the hospital was my new mission field. As long as God had me there, I figured He had me there for a purpose that was bigger than my health. I prayed for and sought out opportunities to witness to hospital staff and other patients.

During one of my stem cell transplants, I spoke with a nurse named Jeanie through the entire procedure. She told me she had once believed in God, but after a bad marriage, she had stopped believing. She used to read the Bible, but now it seemed to her like a fairy tale. I encouraged her to read the Gospel of John and ask God to speak to her and reveal Himself to her. I kept emphasizing how much God loves her and that He is not condemning her. I told her the story of the Prodigal Son and how the father in the story pictures God's love for her. She was really listening to my words, and she told me she hopes Jesus will come back soon.

Another nurse, a 24-year-old Romanian woman named Simona, is a Christian. She confided in me about her struggle in holding out for the right man to marry. She said many of the young Romanian Christian men who had come to America were now going after more money, cars and Hollywood-style girls. She was feeling left out. I prayed for her and she thanked me for encouraging her. There are so many people who need encouragement, and they need to know that God loves them.

I've had numerous near-death experiences through my years of struggling with cancer. The kids and grandkids have all gathered around me to say their last goodbyes, only to find me rebounding sooner or later. On one occasion, I was feeling very tired and was about to lie down for a ten-minute "power nap," but feeling strangely light-headed, I decided to drive myself to the emergency room. As I was checking in, one of the nurses saw me and said, "This man needs blood!"

They infused me with nineteen pints of blood over the next few days. I had a perforated intestine and my blood had been slowly bleeding out. The doctor told me if I had taken that power nap, I would have never woken up again.

So how much more time do I have to run the race that is set before me? I don't know. God knows the days that are ordained for me, so I am not looking at a clock. I am looking instead for more opportunities to share the love of Christ with others.

I used to think that when I prayed for strength, God would make me strong. But God doesn't make me strong. He makes me realize my weakness so that I will rely on His strength. As He promised me years ago, He has been my Helper and He has held my hand. When I am weak, He is strong.

29
A Glimpse of His Glory

I am lying on a hospital bed at the Oregon Health Science University in Portland. My immune system has weakened again due to a very low count of white blood cells and I have been hit with pneumonia once again. The myeloma cells keep multiplying and have spread throughout my body. I am anemic and I feel tired all the time. I've been treated with medications and transfusions, but I don't know how long the Lord will keep me in this body. I don't think I will recover this time.

But facing death, I am also facing Jesus, and so my lowest point has become my highest point. When I remember how faithful He has been to me, and His steadfast commitment to finishing the good work He started in me, I give Him thanks and I worship Him. I have ceased striving against death. My heart is joyful and my soul is still. I know that my God reigns. Just as He has promised, He will be exalted among the nations. He will be exalted in all the earth.

Jesus promised to build His church. He just didn't say exactly how He would do it. If it were up to me, I wouldn't have chosen the church in Liberia to bless the nations. I would have begun in a healthy nation and with a healthy church, not a broken, weak body. But He still chooses foolish things to confound the wise, the things that are not to nullify the things that are. This is apparently why He also chose to use me to start the Romans Project there. I am a lot like Liberia – weak and hopelessly broken. I wouldn't have chosen myself as His servant. I am not a gifted leader. Like Moses, I am not eloquent of speech. But God chose him and He has chosen me. When He met with Moses in the wilderness, He showed up in an ordinary bush. Any old bush would do. God loves using ordinary people to fulfill His purposes.

I feel as though I am looking ahead toward the Promised Land. God has shown me a glimpse of His glory. He has done great things in improbable places, and I know that the best is yet to come. But that is not for me to see. I have finished my race. God gave Moses a right-hand man named Joshua to carry on the mission. He has given to me many different Joshua's. I am not mightily gifted, but He has given me a gift for recognizing those who are. I've just tried to build up and encourage God's key men. Wherever I have spotted them, He has given me the grace to say, "He must increase, and I must decrease."

God has brought all of this together. There has never been a

I long to see Jesus and kneel at His feet, worshiping Him,
my Savior and my God.

meeting of the minds when a lot of gifted people got together and came up with a big strategy for reaching the world. I certainly didn't orchestrate it. God has put together the Romans Project one piece at a time. He is the Lord of the harvest, and He has called laborers into this work by His own choosing. I may be the most unprofitable servant of all. He just gave me one simple question to keep asking Him: "Where are your key men?" And then He answered the question. Sometimes the answer was hiding in plain sight, and the Lord would show me a faithful man that I had not even considered. Other times, I had to go out of my way to find a faithful man. But I learned to recognize His man.

One of the Liberian pastors I first challenged to do the Romans Project is named Jonah Smith. He was sold on it from the start. As they say, your best salesman is a satisfied customer, so Jonah started encouraging his pastor friends to join him in doing the Romans Project. He called me one day and said a pastor from Sierra Leone was visiting him. His name was Daniel. They had met when Jonah was a refugee there. Daniel was very interested in what Jonah had been telling him. He wanted to start reading and copying Romans, so I got his contact information and soon afterward, through him, we launched into a second country. This connection would not have happened if not for the war and for all the refugees who had fled from Liberia to Sierra Leone. It didn't come out of a strategy session. It was something only God could accomplish.

We had sent another young man, Boaki Harleyson, on scholarship to the JETS seminary in Jos, Nigeria. I spoke with him about the Romans Project and he started doing it. He got so enthused, he told some professors there about it and they asked for fifty MP3 players to give out to the seminary students and some church leaders in Jos. We want to give away the MP3's, but only to those who have completed the reading and the copying assignment. With this model in mind, we were then in three countries.

Within a year the Romans Project had spread to Ghana, and then it jumped across the continent to Uganda, Ethiopia, Kenya,

Tanzania, Zimbabwe and Rwanda. It was all God's doing. Most of the connections came to us from people hearing about it by word-of-mouth. English is spoken in all these countries. We then began asking the Lord what He had in mind for the French-speaking countries of Africa. Guinea is a Francophone country. A pastor there who speaks both English and French asked how he could get involved in the Romans Project. He said he knows many other bi-lingual pastors in Guinea. So this began our ministry there.

Within a couple years we were also hearing from pastors and missionaries in the Philippines, India and China. By then, we had delivered nearly 7,000 MP3 players. We were planning for 10,000, but then that number started to seem like it was too low. The goal was bumped to 100,000, but then the simple math started to add up to far more than that. According to Operation Mobilization, there are at least 500,000 untrained pastors in Africa. The number actually may be closer to a million. But if each of those half-million pastors represents a church where we could reward four MP3 players to four faithful church leaders, this would mean at least two million players.

So here is my dream: I believe the Lord will open the way to bring the Romans Project to at least 500,000 pastors in Africa. This is not a fanciful dream. It is actually a very realistic dream. It may amount to nothing more than faith the size of a mustard seed. I say this because God is able to do exceedingly beyond what I am able to ask or even imagine, according to His power that works in His church.

But I won't be here to see the Lord fulfill this dream. He has raised up other faithful men for this. Dr. Rick Calenberg, a SIM missionary I have known for many years, has agreed to be the international coordinator for the Romans Project. Like me, Rick has a heart for developing church leaders. He has years of missionary experience in Africa. He is also a professor of missions at Dallas Theological Seminary. His worldwide connections are far more extensive than my own. With his gifting, he is able to arrange one-day training conferences to teach Romans Project participants how to use the MP3 players and how to do expository preaching. Rick can take the Romans Project where I believe the Lord wants it to go – to the uttermost parts of the earth. I am learning to let go, and let God.

I've mentioned this before, but I think it's worth stating again that, through the Romans Project, I've seen the missions focus at Southwest Bible Church broaden. Of course, it helps that we are using Scott Gilchrist's teaching, but it is more than that. Southwest is a very far-reaching, evangelistic church with a strong emphasis on solid biblical teaching. This is a reflection of Scott and his ministry staff. Every church has unique features that draw certain people to it. I've always been drawn to a church that has a special emphasis on missions, but at Southwest Bible, the mission emphasis is woven seamlessly into the entire fabric of the church. It doesn't stand out among other features in the church, but it is outstanding. I'll admit, it took me a while to see this. As important as it is for individual believers to abide in the Word in order to bear lasting fruit, it is even more important for an entire church to abide in the Word. The fruit that glorifies God comes from abiding in the Word, not the work. This has always been the main focus at Southwest Bible. Evangelism and missions flow from the heart of a church that is abiding in Christ and His Word.

So in a sense, God has used a healthy church to bless the nations in Africa. The Romans Project is God's gift to the church there and beyond.

God is a cheerful giver. He also gives according to the need of each person in every place. In Africa, a pastor may be a farmer. He may need to walk everywhere he goes. So while he is busy working or walking, he can listen to the teaching on his MP3 player. Faith comes by hearing, and hearing by the Word of Christ. And on this rock, Jesus said he would build His church.

Afterword: Heaven's Door

A Daughter's Perspective

The hospital had sent Dad home. There was no more they could do. His time was near. Dad asked us to come within the next two weeks. He wanted to gather with the whole family to pray and give a blessing to us before he left for his eternal home. I wasn't sure we should wait. We drove to my parent's home that weekend.

We all gathered together on September 16th for what we began to call "The Blessing." Dad was lying on a hospice bed in their living room. Though feverish, he was on a mission! We had no idea the length this time of blessing would take. He began around 10 am with the youngest grandchild and talked to each of the eighteen grandchildren, assuring them of his love and challenging them in areas he was concerned about or in things he wanted them to consider. Meanwhile his fever continued to rise, so one of us kept a cool washcloth on his forehead or his feet to try to keep him cooler. Then he talked with each of the daughters alongside her husband. Last of all he spoke with Mom. Each one went up to his bed and sat next to him while he spoke to them and prayed for them. In that there was no longer any reason to keep germs away, we could hug our dear dad and grandpa. Many tears were shed. He challenged the older grandkids to take time with the younger ones since he wouldn't be there to encourage them to draw closer to Jesus. "Marry only someone who truly loves the Lord and His Word." He also cautioned, "Don't get so busy in ministry you forget to spend time with your kids." Each was specific and intentional, with the thought to encourage and motivate. He continued through the evening until one in the morning when all was complete. He was exhausted. He spent close to fifteen hours on his deathbed taking the time to tell us he loved us and pointing us directly to Jesus. What a gift we received from him in his life of real faith in God to his final breaths challenging us to press on to the end, to be faithful to the Lord until we met again in the presence of Jesus.

Near one in the morning after Dad had talked and
prayed with each of us

The next morning Dad woke up a little disappointed. He knew he had done all he could do with this life and he was a little surprised that he was still here. But his time was very close. Two days later he walked into the presence of Jesus.

I have never watched someone die before. Death is a strange door. We are all so close to that door. Most of the time we feel like it is far away, but that day, I saw how close that door was. We aren't meant for death. *Lord, this is one of Your beloved. He has given You his life and here he is struggling for breath. We are giving him medicine to help him, trying to keep the mucous from building up in his throat so he can breathe and yet he is dying. This is a struggle for life against death. A struggle we all lose. And yet in that loss, we get to be with You, because You won. Somehow, even in death, it is obvious You designed us to live.*

Around one in the morning on the 19th we called my other sisters and they were quickly on their way. He was struggling to breathe. I got on the phone with the hospice nurses. We couldn't figure out how to help him. We weren't trained. We didn't know what we were doing. *It doesn't seem like the right kind of grand finale for one who is Yours, Lord.* And yet that is how we all go. There is no grand finale. We just have to walk through a door. He wouldn't have wanted a grand finale focused on him, but somehow when you love someone and see all they have done and given, you feel they deserve something more than struggling to breathe and then death. Jesus had so much more for him. It just wasn't here. It was with Him and we had to say goodbye.

While I was talking with the nurse I saw my dad transition to final breaths. I had never seen this before, but I knew. My sisters saw it happening too. He was leaving us! I interrupted the nurse, realizing, there was nothing more we could do - "I gotta go! My dad is walking into the presence of Jesus! I gotta go!" I hung up the phone and we held his hands, singing *When We All Get to Heaven* and watched him breathe his last. Our dad walked into the very presence of Jesus. No more pain, no more suffering, but more than that, he was with Jesus, his Lord and Savior, his Creator, his God. How could I ever sing the songs about seeing Jesus face to face again without weeping in memory of the reality we have of walking into the presence of Jesus, no matter what kind of death we face here on this planet. Heaven with Jesus, through death's door, became a very real and close door to us. It is only a breath away.

We woke Mom, who had lain down to rest, telling her of Dad's passing. "Oh that is wonderful! How wonderful for him, for sure. Home with Jesus!" Sitting in their living room, we enjoyed a time of sharing, tears and joy at his passing into his heavenly home.

"Precious in the sight of the Lord is the death of His saints."[26] Dad's departure is precious to the Lord, almost like a new birth into eternity, but it wrenches our hearts. The weight of realizing there would never be a conversation on this earth with Dad began to settle in, but he still had something to say. Even in his last days Dad sought to move past the despairing days of suffering and invest in the generations following. Tucked inside the safe at Mom and Dad's house was his final gift. Six months prior to his death, he had set out to secretly write a biblical blessing on specially chosen stationery to each grandchild, daughter, son-in-law, and Mom. Typed on each personal page was that person's name, the meaning of that name, things Dad appreciated about each one and an exhortation along with Bible verses. "I have gone on to Jesus, but if you walk with Him, we will see each other again. Until then, be faithful to the Lord."

He gave a unique and precious gift from his heart to ours. Some read theirs over and over. Others wept when receiving it. I read it once and put it away for about three years. It has taken a while for our hearts to heal after the loss. Jesus understands the loss and separation. But the loss isn't forever. It is only for a short time. Some day we will see Jesus and He will wipe away every tear from our eyes and welcome us who love Him home.

Postscript: Romans Project
Jim Morud

John and Jeanette Corey and their daughters were twice chased out of Africa by war. In both Ethiopia and Liberia, they held out leaving until the last possible moment, diligently working to prepare church leaders to withstand the mayhem that would inevitably tear apart their countries and their churches. After a long and valiant fight with cancer, John went to heaven on September 19, 2012. He was an ordinary man whose legacy reflects his resolute spirit. The Romans Project is a simple plan for helping tens of thousands of pastors and church leaders to walk in the truth through hard times as John also had done.

While Africa is now rising in many respects, nearly half of its 53 nations are currently embroiled in some kind of conflict. Age-old tribal and religious hostilities and bloody revolutions go on and on. But the enduring difference John and Jeanette brought to Africa is the hope that Jesus Christ can still save war-weary people, even from themselves.

Over twenty years ago, nearly a million Tutsis were massacred in Rwanda by the majority Hutu tribe. Shortly after the genocide had halted, a memorial museum was erected outside of Kigali, the capital city. The words of an 11-year-old boy named Donata, a war orphan, were inscribed on a plaque: *"Sometimes I get very sad because I can't imagine what my life will be like. I will never see my parents again, and yet I will see the people who killed them, and those people's children, for the rest of my life. I can't bear the thought of it."*

As with most of the nations of Africa, the birth and growth of the African church has also come with many pangs.

"I was not able to fully forgive until I met Jesus," said Rwandan Romans Project coordinator, Albert Mabasi, a Tutsi. Albert shares the horrific memories of young Donata and millions of his countrymen, but he has found in the love of Christ a power to help heal his country and to move on from the past. The church in Rwanda is comprised of both Tutsis and Hutu. Albert is now urging pastors and church leaders of both tribes to reconcile by taking God's truth to heart through the Romans Project.

Gahini is a dusty village perched on a high hill in Eastern Rwanda. It is the original site of the legendary East Africa Revival Movement of the early 1930's, which also birthed a Christian missionary hospital that has treated thousands of people plagued with HIV. Sensing the need for spiritual revival and healing to again come to Rwanda, more than a hundred pastors attended a recent Romans Project conference in Gahini, some walking for over an hour to get there. After the conference, they walked back to their villages committed to reading and writing Romans. Their MP3 players were loaded with solid biblical teaching that will aid them in their journey toward the revival they are seeking.

To the east of Rwanda, in Uganda, another nation that is acquainted with horrific atrocities, the Romans Project is collaborating with Proclaim-Africa to empower church leaders with the Word of God. When first told about the simple Romans Project plan, many pastors are surprised by its simplicity. Proclaim-Africa senior staff leader, Allan Koki, marveled, saying, "I had never thought of this." But the beauty and the staying power of the Romans Project is actually in its simplicity, rooted in God's Word.

Africa today is fertile ground for revival, and seed planted in rich soil springs to life. The Romans Project has now spread to fifteen African nations, including over 13,000 pastors and has also gone into India and the Philippines. Most of this growth has come purely by word-of-mouth, the usual manner by which news still travels in Africa. Among the 823 scriptural expository messages contained on the MP3 player, Scott Gilchrist's teaching from the Book of Romans and much of the Gospel of Luke has been translated into French, Amharic, Oromo, Swahili, Luo, Luganda, Tigrinya, Hausa, Kinyarwanda and counting.

God is using ordinary, committed servants, like John Corey, to spread the Romans Project. Bonheur is the Romans Project director in the Congo. He is a humble but brilliant young man who speaks nine languages, even without any formal education. He fell in love with the gospel while he was doing the required reading and writing of Romans following a conference he attended in Rwanda. But he was skeptical of how it would be received by other Congo clerics. Years after the Second Congo War, in which more than five million of his countrymen had lost their lives, Congolese church leaders were still estranged from one another. But with the prospect of earning an MP3 player by reading and writing Romans, many attended a Romans Project conference in Brazzaville. Bonheur, neither trained nor ordained, asked the pastors if they loved each other, according to Romans 12-14. By the end of the conference the pastors began confessing their animosities and were on their knees praying together, repenting and asking God to heal their hearts, their churches and their land. The leaders of the largest denominations in the Congo are now the biggest advocates of the Romans Project.

When church leaders' hearts and lives are changed, their congregations follow their lead. In many cases, the change has meant that pastors have actually come to faith in Christ by reading Romans. Said Julius, a pastor in Accra, Ghana, "After reading the Book of Romans, I am now fully convinced that I am saved by grace through faith in Christ, nothing more or less. This knowledge has changed my method of preaching."

Five hundred years ago, Martin Luther came to the same understanding by reading Romans. This revelation changed the course of church history, which changed the world. Today in

Africa, thousands of church leaders are reading, writing and studying the same truths, sparking revival in their churches.

Pastor Moses, a leading pastor in Nigeria, said, "I am having a wonderful time reading Romans twenty times. It is a great spiritual experience for me. It is so encouraging, reading and playing the messages of the book (Romans). I am enjoying it so much, and am teaching it in my church. When I get up in the morning I read. At night I read, and any time I can get I am reading Romans. I am encouraging the people of my church to be reading it. Everywhere I go, people see me with the earphones in and ask me about it. I tell them how wonderful it is."

John and Jeanette Corey left Ethiopia and Liberia in tears, but sowing in tears, they left African leaders behind them to reap in gladness.

Appendix

What is the Romans Project?

Most of the world's evangelical church leaders have little access to solid theological resources. Quality seminaries are hundreds of miles away from remote churches and travel is expensive and sometimes dangerous. Computers and internet access—even electricity—are luxuries which many cannot afford.

With new congregations forming daily, the global church is quickly growing. Traditional methods such as Bible schools and seminaries for equipping church leaders cannot keep up with this rapid growth rate. The good news is that there is a real hunger for good, solid Bible teaching. Unfortunately, a staggering number – 18.7 million evangelical churches in the world today – are being led by men and women with no theological training.

How can these church leaders get the solid Biblical training they need to teach their congregations about the life-transforming, foundational truths of the gospel of Jesus Christ? The book of Romans in the Bible is a great place to start!

Our Mission

To equip pastors to abide in and feed their congregations from God's Word.

The Challenge to Pastors

Read

We challenge pastors to immerse themselves in God's Word by committing to read the Book of Romans twenty times.

Write

We have found that hand copying the Scriptures is a valuable method for slowly abiding in and acquiring a deeper understanding of God's Word. Pastors are challenged to write out their own copy of the Book of Romans. As they do so, the great truths of the gospel of Jesus Christ take deep root in their hearts.

Listen

After the reading and writing challenge is complete, participants receive an Mp3 player loaded with a full exposition of Romans. The Mp3 player includes an overview of Romans in 18 expositional messages, as well as a thorough, in-depth study of Romans in 109 expositions. On the same portable player, we have included verse-by-verse expositions of other books of the Bible, including John, Acts, Genesis, and Luke.

As pastors and leaders learn for themselves the benefits from their time of reading, writing and listening to Romans, we encourage them to continue on and do similar studies in other books of the Bible. In this way, they not only are learning for themselves, but they are able to pass on what they are learning to their congregations.

If you would like to know more about the Romans Project or would like to participate, check us out at www.romansproject.org.

Jim Morud

Most of us can't see the significance of our own stories. Even as followers of Jesus, who is the author of our faith, we tend to forget, or don't even really believe, that He is relentlessly writing a good story over our ordinary lives. We get all too familiar with our own familiarity. So God gives storytellers to us to help us see the good stories that are hidden in the everyday. Jim Morud has this gift. He's been sifting and sorting and crafting stories of God's inscription on human hearts for nearly forty years. As a foreign correspondent for the ministry of CRU, Jim shook the bushes and found some fascinating stories in unlikely places around the globe. And so his trained eye made him the right person for probing and telling John Corey's story, *Any Ol' Bush Will Do.* Jim traveled with John during three of his mission trips to Russia. He saw and heard and felt the impact of John's life and ministry on the people he served there. And then when John was facing death, he interviewed him to keep his remarkable story from slipping untold into eternity. Jim lives with his wife, Linda, and four children in Warren, Oregon, where he continues to write more stories he has shaken from the bushes.

Jim with John, preparing for a conference in Kavalerovo, Russia

[1] NASB, 2 Timothy 4:6-8,
[2] Ibid., Proverbs 16:9.
[3] Ibid., Luke 18:22
[4] Ibid., James 2:18
[5] KJV, Proverbs 24:27,
[6] NASB, Proverbs 15:1
[7] Ibid.
[8] Isaiah 32:17 KJV
[9] Ibid., Psalm 34:3
[10] NKJV, Revelation 3:20
[11] Ibid., Hebrews 13:5
[12] ibid., 2 Timothy 2:3
[13] Ibid., Hebrews 13:6
[14] NASB, Psalm 121:7-8
[15] Ibid., Isaiah 8:12-13
[16] KJV, Psalm 46:10a
[17] Ibid., Psalm 46:10
[18] NIV, Philippians 1:23,
[19] Ibid., Philippians 1:24
[20] KJV., Psalm 46:10
[21] NASB, Exodus 20:5-6
[22] NIV, Deuteronomy 6:2
[23] NASB., 2 Corinthians 12:9a
[24] Ibid., 2 Corinthians 12:9b
[25] Ibid., Isaiah 41:13
[26] NKJV Psalms 116:15